More Praise for *Yoga Wisdom at Work*

"A significant contribution to the body of literature bridging East and West, the Showkeirs' work provides a powerful guide for applying the principles of yoga to develop human potential and enhance work satisfaction. Highly recommended."
—**Howard Cutler, coauthor of the bestselling** *The Art of Happiness* **(with the Dalai Lama)**

"This generous, insightful, and eminently practical book is offered with an open heart from years of experience—the best practice manual I've read for how to embody authenticity and integrity. I am grateful to Maren and Jamie for bringing together the disciplines of yoga and leadership."
—**Meg Wheatley, bestselling author of** *Leadership and the New Science* **and** *So Far from Home*

"With so much emphasis these days on practicing poses, the other seven limbs of yoga are often overlooked. The application of ancient wisdom to modern life situations offered here will be helpful to all people, whether or not they ever set foot on a yoga mat. Please read this book!"
—**Desirée Rambaugh, internationally known master yoga teacher**

"Translating this essential, ancient knowledge into a pragmatic, contemporary context is a huge and valuable contribution. Expand your knowledge and expand your life with this book!"
—**Kevin Cashman, bestselling author of** *Leadership from the Inside Out* **and** *The Pause Principle*

"The Showkeirs draw upon 2,000-year-old wisdom and adroitly weave personal stories and case histories to crisply illustrate the Eight Limbs of Yoga's applications in the contemporary workplace."
—**Dr. Paul Mittman, president and CEO, Southwest College of Naturopathic Medicine and Health Sciences**

"By relating all aspects of yoga to the workplace and using everyday language, the authors put the intricacies of this advanced spiritual tradition within reach of the general public....a useful tool for those seeking to expand their understanding and practice of yoga whether they are experienced yoga practitioners or have just begun their first class."
—**Anna Jedrziewski, book reviewer, *Retailing Insight* (formerly *New Age Retailer*)**

"I love the book's simple, clear instructions on how to infuse your daily work life with ancient spiritual principles and practices. Rather than rolling up your sanity in a yoga mat, you can keep it by practicing yoga at work. All together now: 'Ommmmm.' Perfect!"
—**BJ Gallagher, bestselling coauthor of *A Peacock in the Land of Penguins* and *Being Buddha at Work***

YOGA
WISDOM
AT WORK

Also by

Jamie Showkeir and Maren Showkeir

Authentic Conversations:
Moving from Manipulations
to Truth and Commitment

YOGA
WISDOM
AT WORK

FINDING SANITY
OFF THE MAT AND ON THE JOB

Maren Showkeir and Jamie Showkeir

Berrett–Koehler Publishers, Inc.
San Francisco
a BK Life book

Berrett-Koehler Publishers, Inc.
235 Montgomery Street, Suite 650, San Francisco, CA 94104-2916
Tel: (415) 288-0260   Fax: (415) 362-2512   www.bkconnection.com

Ordering Information

Quantity sales. Special discounts are available on quantity purchases by corporations, associations, and others. For details, contact the "Special Sales Department" at the Berrett-Koehler address above.

Individual sales. Berrett-Koehler publications are available through most bookstores. They can also be ordered directly from Berrett-Koehler: Tel: (800) 929-2929; Fax: (802) 864-7626; www.bkconnection.com

Orders for college textbook/course adoption use. Please contact Berrett-Koehler: Tel: (800) 929-2929; Fax: (802) 864-7626.

Orders by U.S. trade bookstores and wholesalers. Please contact Ingram Publisher Services, Tel: (800) 509-4887; Fax: (800) 838-1149; E-mail: customer. service@ingrampublisher services.com; or visit www.ingrampublisherservices.com/ Ordering for details about electronic ordering.

Berrett-Koehler and the BK logo are registered trademarks of Berrett-Koehler Publishers, Inc.

Printed in the United States of America

Berrett-Koehler books are printed on long-lasting acid-free paper. When it is available, we choose paper that has been manufactured by environmentally responsible processes. These may include using trees grown in sustainable forests, incorporating recycled paper, minimizing chlorine in bleaching, or recycling the energy produced at the paper mill.

Library of Congress Cataloging-in-Publication Data

Showkeir, Maren, 1957–

Yoga wisdom at work : finding sanity off the mat and on the job / Maren Showkeir & Jamie Showkeir. — First edition.

    pages cm

Summary: "Yoga practitioners fight work stress with stretching and breathing exercises—but does yoga stop when you step off the mat? In this surprising book, the authors show why poses—*asanas*—are just one part of yoga practice. There are seven other "limbs" of yoga that are often neglected, especially during the workday"—Provided by publisher.

ISBN 978-1-60994-797-2 (pbk.)

1. Hatha yoga. 2. Yoga—Philosophy. 3. Mind and body. I. Showkeir, Jamie, 1952– II. Title.

RA781.7.S477 2013

613.7'046—dc23   2012047352

First Edition

18 17 16 15 14 13   10 9 8 7 6 5 4 3 2 1

Interior design/art: Laura Lind Design   Edit: Lunaea Weatherstone
Coverdesign: Susan Malikowski, Designleaf Studio Proofread: Henri Bensussen
Production service: Linda Jupiter Productions   Index: Linda Webster

CONTENTS

Foreword by Christine Day   vii

Note to Our Readers   ix

INTRODUCTION: Work and the Yogic Path   1

ONE: Beginner's Mind: The Power and the Promise   11

TWO: The First Limb: Universal Morality   21
The *Yamas*   22
  NON-VIOLENCE (*AHIMSA*)   23
  NON-LYING (*SATYA*)   35
  NON-STEALING (*ASTEYA*)   47
  NON-SQUANDERING OF VITAL ENERGIES
  (*BRAHMACHARYA*)   55
  NON-GREED (*APARIGRAHA*)   63

THREE: The Second Limb: Personal Code of Conduct   73
The *Niyamas*   74
  PURITY (*SAUCHA*)   76
  CONTENTMENT (*SANTOSHA*)   83
  DISCIPLINE (*TAPAS*)   94
  SELF-STUDY (*SVADHYAYA*)   101
  SURRENDER (*ISHVARA-PRANIDHANA*)   112

FOUR: The Third Limb: Postures (*Asana*)   121

FIVE: The Fourth Limb: Breath Control (*Pranayama*)   131
  Pranayama Techniques   **139**

SIX: The Fifth Limb: Withdrawal of the Senses
(*Pratyahara*)   141

SEVEN: The Sixth Limb: Focus (*Dharana*)   151

EIGHT: The Seventh Limb: Meditation (*Dhyana*)   161

NINE: The Eighth Limb: Absorption (*Samadhi*)   171

CONCLUSION: Finding Your Way   183

Glossary of Terms   191

Resources   193

Acknowledgments   196

Index   198

About the Authors   206

About *hennings-showkeir & associates, inc.*   209

FOREWORD

Lululemon is often described as a "yoga-inspired" athletic-apparel company because much of our business model is dedicated to serving the needs of yoga practitioners. However, that same phrase could apply to so much more than the products we offer. Yoga inspires the way we treat our employees, our customers, our investors, and our communities. Those who do not practice yoga might underestimate the quiet energy and focus that it can provide to individuals and companies, both. I can speak for my colleagues in saying that we do not view yoga as something that only happens in a class, after which we return to the "real world." As Maren and Jamie Showkeir ably point out in this book, yoga is more a philosophy and a way of life than just another type of exercise. You do not have to be on a yoga mat to practice yoga.

Many businesspeople marvel at lululemon's "decentralized" structure and abhorrence of micromanagement. Our store managers, for example, are empowered to make decisions for their unique stores and to take risks without "checking with corporate." After reading this book, you'll understand why such a work culture makes perfect sense for a yoga-inspired company. Does this thinking lead to a lack of responsibility, focus, or alignment? Absolutely not! We often speak of "relaxing into a pose" in yoga, or "creating space," and yet find that we can achieve so much more when we do not try to establish rigid control over the body. I don't need to tell you that yoga is not for the fainthearted or for those who are not interested in reaching their highest potential—one reason we emphasize yoga practice in our hiring process, often asking applicants to join us for yoga class! The discipline of yoga provides a wonderful framework for bringing our best selves and talents to work, yet also giving us the space to recognize our doubts and limitations.

Yoga never asks us to be somebody we're not (how many of us stubbornly insist on competing with others in yoga class even so!), yet it does call us to be everything we can be. I can say exactly the same thing about lululemon as a workplace. I heartily commend Maren and Jamie for describing the wonderful gifts that yoga can bring to the workday. I believe, as they believe, that work is life, too. To paraphrase the lululemon manifesto, "This is not your practice life; this is all there is."

Christine Day
Vancouver, British Columbia

For all the teachers,

for their teachers' teachers,

and most especially for ours,

Mary Bruce

NOTE TO OUR READERS

This was written in the first person, in the voice of Maren, for reasons of clarity, coherence, and to minimize confusion. Though it reads as if emanating from a single person, in truth, these words spring from union. This book is the offspring of partnership, both in marriage and business, and represents the combined thinking, conversations, and practices that color our life together.

The stories and anecdotes throughout the book are based on interviews or first-person experiences. Some people were willing to have their names used, while others preferred not to be identified. In the end, we decided that for stories we would use first names for uniformity and so we would not have to interrupt the narrative with "not her/his real name" references. Where surnames are used, these are people's real names.

Our intention and commitment are to accuracy, and we have tried to give full credit to those whose quotes or content we have incorporated into this book. We are eager to correct factual errors or address omissions that readers may find.

Maren and Jamie

The Eight Limbs of Yoga

Union, absorption			SAMADHI		
Meditation			DHYANA		
Focus			DHARANA		
Sense withdrawal			PRATYAHARA		
Breath			PRANAYAMA		
Postures			ASANA		
Personal conduct	**NIYAMAS**				
	Saucha (purity)	Satosha (content)	Svadhyaya (self-study)	Tapas (discipline)	Ishvara-pranidhana (surrender)
Moral code	**YAMAS**				
	Ahimsa (non-violence)	Satya (non-lying)	Asteya (non-stealing)	Brahmacharya (non-waste of vital energies)	Aparigraha (non-greed)

WORK AND THE YOGIC PATH

*Can you coax your mind from its wandering
and keep to the original oneness?*

*Can you let your body become
supple as a newborn child's?*

*Can you cleanse your inner vision
until you see nothing but the light?*

*Can you love people and lead them
without imposing your will?*

*Can you deal with the most vital matters
by letting events take their course?*

*Can you step back from your own mind
and thus understand all things?*

*Giving birth and nourishing,
Having without possessing,
Action with no expectations,
Leading and not trying to control:
This is the supreme virtue.*

Tao Te Ching

Yoga for me began as a mild flirtation. In the beginning, I wasn't all that interested in investing too much in the relationship.

In the late 1980s, I wandered into the world of yoga to extend my physical fitness routine. My goal was muscular flexibility and better balance. The first few classes I took were what most people in the Western world commonly experience: Enter a brightly lit room at a gym, community hall, or studio. Depending on the environment, the session might include a short meditation or a reading designed to center and calm the restless, chattering "monkey mind." We'd plop down on mats and spend an hour or more stretching, breathing, and twisting our bodies into poses with strange-sounding names. Before ending class, the teacher would ask us to recline on the mats for a resting pose called *savasana*.

Just as the instructions to lie down were being given, and before the teacher dimmed the lights for *savasana*, I used to sneak out of yoga class. Resting on the floor for five or ten minutes seemed like a waste of my valuable time when I had so many important things to do at work.

I don't feel that way any more.

WHOLE YOGA, WHOLE WORK

After an initial burst of enthusiasm, my practice sputtered for a few years. But in time, yoga got under my skin in ways I did not even realize. As a more committed practice evolved in the 1990s, it began subtly influencing my lifestyle choices. An example: One day I suddenly realized that my beloved and multidecade Dr Pepper addiction had been broken—I hadn't partaken of any kind of soda for more than a year! Although I never consciously set out to give up my habit of drinking several glasses of cola per day, water had become my first drink of choice. As I analyzed why, it became clear that yoga's emphasis on healthy living had been subconsciously motivational.

By the late 1990s, yoga had become such an important and integral part of my life that I yearned to know more about it. In 2005, when I was at a personal and professional crossroads, I took the opportunity to enroll in a 200-hour yoga teacher-training course taught by Mary Bruce in Tempe, Arizona. This was the beginning of a fruitful journey that has helped me better understand and appreciate the full spectrum of a yoga practice, and the benefits it has to offer in daily living and at work. And the journey continues.

Although I try to live my life without regrets, I often wish I had discovered this practice at a much younger age. In particular, it would have been so useful to discover the knowledge contained in all Eight Limbs of Yoga, which goes far beyond the most common practice of doing poses on a mat. A deeper, broader practice would have enhanced every aspect of my life—but most especially at work.

Looking back at my professional life, 20/20 hindsight tells me that incorporating yoga practices and philosophies early on would have helped me better serve the people I worked with and the enterprises that employed me. Had I embraced its moral constructs, understood the power of recognizing and developing my potential and that of others, I would have been a more productive worker, a more skillful manager, and a more effective leader.

YOGA'S TRANSFORMATIVE INFLUENCE

My decision to enroll in yoga teacher training in the fall of 2005 coincided with a resolution to leave the newspaper industry for good. Although I had thoroughly enjoyed this rollercoaster of a career for more than twenty years, a gentle and persuasive inner voice had been insisting for several months that it was time for something new.

Another new adventure began simultaneously with my yoga teacher training—working with Jamie Showkeir (now my husband and business partner) as an organizational consultant. As I began learning about Jamie's work philosophy and approach to helping organizations become more successful, we both were blown away by how yoga principles dovetailed beautifully with concepts he considered foundational to his consulting work. Both my new career and a deepened yoga practice were giving me language to articulate things that long had been imbedded in my own philosophical views about work.

When I returned from yoga teacher-training classes, Jamie and I would have rich, animated conversations about how yoga was complementing and supplementing the work we were doing together. Jamie began doing yoga with me, and it worked a subtle magic on him as well.

Our first book, *Authentic Conversations*, was influenced by our yoga practice, both in content and creation. We did a weeklong yoga retreat with Mary in Troncones Beach, Mexico, and set intentions around writing the book through a guided meditation practice called yoga *nidra*. A few days later, we were in Mount Shasta, California, sequestered in our friends' house to begin the project. I went into that cozy house with a lot of reservations about writing and editing with someone who was both beloved husband and business partner, but it turned out to be a charmed, rewarding experience. Our writing days began with meditation, which helped keep us focused, centered, and compassionate toward each other. We wrote a solid first draft in eight days.

Yoga has continued to influence the way we work together every day. Jamie and I began seriously exploring the ideas for a second book soon after I earned my master's degree in Human and Organizational Development. About the same time, I enrolled in a series of yoga Master Immersion Classes with Mary and Lynn Matthews, of Yoga4Life, based in Baltimore. This sparked happy memories of those early days of being immersed in yoga teacher training and the useful knowledge and skills I had incorporated into a new career. Slowly, the seed of an idea that had lain dormant in my head for a few years began to germinate. I visualized a book about the ways that taking yoga "off the mat" and into the workplace could give people tools to be more successful and sane in high-stress environments.

A FRESH FRAME FOR ANCIENT WISDOM

In our consulting work, we often encounter the term "thought leader." The definition is a little fuzzy, depending on perspective and context. It typically is bestowed on someone viewed as a visionary or futurist, or a person who has laid claim to development of a fresh, breakthrough product or a countercultural business model.

For those looking to differentiate themselves in a crowded, global marketplace, the term can be utilitarian. At the same time, if you consider that human discovery, innovation, and creativity don't spring from a black hole with a proverbial Big Bang, the term is a bit equivocal.

What people call "new" or "innovative" always is built upon historical exploration, discovery, and experience. The world's knowledge base has grown exponentially, and now is so vast and deep that trying to keep up with the pace of change can cause vertigo. Even Patanjali, the Indian sage often called the Father of Yoga, only codified ancient teachings and traditions that had existed for generations. Called the Sutras, his foundational yoga text (estimated to have been written between 500 BCE and 100 BCE) formalized a "new" way to study yoga, yet Patanjali created it from the contributions of masters who practiced, taught, and wrote before him.

So it is with this book. These pages intend to reflect the wisdom of the ancient masters and teachers, and the teachers who came after them, and those who came after them. In the words of yoga master Sri K. Pattabhi Jois, who died in 2009: "Yoga is a way of life and philosophy. It can be practiced by anyone with an inclination to undertake it, for yoga belongs to humanity as a whole. It is not the property of any one group or any one individual, but can be followed by any and all, in any corner of the globe, regardless of class, creed or religion."

PRACTICING YOGA OFF THE MAT

What we humbly offer here is a framework and an invitation to consider applying this wisdom to your work life. Our intention is to explore the broad practice of yoga with a practical focus on its great potential to influence how you engage work to become more successful, satisfied, *and* serene.

This book is based partly on the fact that yoga precepts in the Eight Limbs are beautifully aligned with the principles and philosophies Jamie and I use in our work. Like yoga does, we emphasize precepts such as setting clear intentions, telling the truth (with goodwill), individual accountability for the collective, and the importance of self-awareness. Another reason we wrote the book is that most people have at least heard of yoga, or do a physical practice, or know someone who does. Because yoga and meditation have become such familiar and popular activities in the Western world, we see an opportunity for filtering those precepts through the lens of our expertise in workplace culture.

Our goal is to shed light on a beautiful tool for uncovering your potential and enriching your experience on the job. Yoga has great potency for helping you alter your perspective about the purpose of work, the people you work with, and the organizations you work in.

Yoga's popularity in the West began growing slowly after Swami Vivekananda introduced it in the United States in 1893 at the Parliament of Religions in Chicago. It attracted followers in the next 100 years, getting a boost from the publicity generated when the Beatles studied with the Maharishi Mahesh Yogi in the 1960s. By the mid-1990s (about the time I began practicing), the number of practitioners was estimated to be about 5 million, and that number had more than tripled to 18 million by 2008. Even so, Yogarupa Rod Stryker, a nationally known yogi and our teacher's teacher, observes that while yoga's popularity in the U.S. has exploded, a full recognition of the richness of its potential benefits remains obscure. "We've reduced the spectrum of what [yoga] can be, how it can benefit us," he says.

Jamie and I do not see ourselves as yoga "experts"—we want to be emphatic about that. I have studied yoga for more than fifteen years. I have a committed practice and a few hundred hours of teacher training. Jamie has had a meditation practice since the 1970s and developed an *asana* practice in 2005. The more we learn, the clearer it becomes that we have so much more to learn.

Our intention here is not to turn you into a yoga expert or a scholar who can translate Sanskrit and recite verses from Patanjali's Sutras or other yogic sacred texts. Like all yoga students, we rely on talented, dedicated teachers to help us stretch—literally and metaphorically. Among other things, doing yoga is an ever-present reminder about the importance of humility and the value of fostering a beginner's mind.

Having said that, we have decades of experience in improving workplace environments and collaborating with others to develop human potential. Our expertise is rooted in helping people in organizations understand the business benefits of harmonizing the need for achieving successful business results with finding meaning and purpose at work. Our point of view is in tune with the ancient philosophies and concepts in the Eight Limbs, which offer a guide for enhancing contribution to the greater good, increasing well-being, and fostering a calm, focused mind. These qualities and more will benefit your work life.

What we propose in this book is a journey of exploration and discovery. The seats of the teacher and the student are the same. Our primary intention is to help you stretch in the way others have helped us.

THE ROADMAP

Yoga contains no commandments, nor is it associated with religion or dogma. In teacher-training classes, the adage "one well of truth, and many paths" is invoked often, to signify that each individual travels a unique path of self-discovery on the way to the well of wisdom, fulfillment, and enlightenment.

Although references to God or Lord are plentiful in yoga scriptures and literature, how one interprets God is fluid and up to the individual. We know dedicated yoga practitioners who are devout in the beliefs of their chosen religions or traditions. On the other end of the spectrum, we know committed yogis who are agnostic or atheists. The late Eknath Easwaran, a yogi, spiritual teacher, and founder of the Blue Mountain Center of Meditation in northern California, addressed this in one of his numerous books, *Conquest of the Mind*: "If you believe in a personal God, ask for the help of Sri Krishna or Jesus or the Divine Mother. . . . If you do not believe in a personal God, ask for help from your own deeper Self, the Atman. Either way, it is important to remember that you are appealing to a power deep within you, not to anyone outside."

For the purpose of this book, yoga is set forth as a practice that will help you discover your own spark of divinity, which we define as human and spiritual potential. The Sanskrit meaning of the word yoga is "yoke" or "union." The ability to look inward, recognize and acknowledge your potential, then develop that in a way that unites it with your highest, divine self—that is yoga. It also asks that you recognize that boundless potential in others. This perspective is contained in the traditional yoga salutation *namasté*, which translates into "my soul recognizes and bows to the divinity of yours."

Yoga does not provide answers. Pema Chodron, Buddhist nun, author, and teacher, says it is important to realize that ". . . no slogan, no meditation practice, nothing that you can hear in the teachings is a solution. We're evolving. We will always be learning more and more, continually opening further and further." What yoga does offer is a guide for discovering the light that exists within you and always has. It urges you to unveil your brilliance to the world and to recognize the light that also burns in others. This luminescence reveals that you are perfect as you are. With steadfast practice, yoga leads you to that realization.

The lake of potential is always there, shimmering within you. You may not acknowledge that it exists, but that doesn't make it disappear. Perhaps you see it but prefer to stay safely on shore. Maybe you're willing to wade in partway. With a dedicated practice, yoga can give you the confidence to take a screaming, joyful leap into its depths. Once you realize it contains what you need to achieve satisfaction and success, playing it safe is like choosing to be a spectator of your own life.

Whatever regrets Jamie and I may have about not having found yoga sooner have been banished by remembering this: it is never too late to begin.

one

BEGINNER'S MIND:
THE POWER AND THE PROMISE

Yoga has less to do with what you can do with your body or with being able to still your mind than it has to do with the happiness that unfolds from realizing your full potential.

Yogarupa Rod Stryker

M ore often than we can count, people have said to us, "I could never do yoga. I'm not flexible" (or "I'm too hyper"). That logic is like saying, "I can't tend to my garden—it has too many weeds in it." Or to use a work metaphor, "I can't clean out my email inbox. It has too many messages in it."

It's understandable. The sheer amount of *stuff* we are asked to attend to in our daily lives can be overwhelming. But when people say they lack the physicality to put their bodies into yoga poses, they are not taking into account that it is *the practice* that develops flexibility, balance, and a quiet mind.

In any case, yoga on the mat is only one part of the practice—one-eighth, to be exact. To use one of Jamie's favorite analogies, the physical practice (*asana*) doesn't represent the spectrum of yoga any more than looking through a knothole in a fence and seeing a pitcher throw and catch a ball gives you a complete picture of a baseball game's nine innings. Renowned Swiss psychologist Carl Jung, who received an honorary degree from the University of Calcutta, said, "Yoga practice would be ineffectual without the concepts on which yoga is based. It combines the bodily and the spiritual in an extraordinarily complete way."

The first time I heard a yoga teacher mention the "Eight Limbs of Yoga," I was a mid-career newspaper journalist, and the term sounded bizarre to me. I imagined some exotic Hindu deity with appendages sprouting from its body like an octopus. Although I had taken a few yoga classes at that time, I knew almost nothing about the provenance or philosophical underpinnings of this rich, ancient tradition. While the teacher's brief description of the Eight Limbs sounded interesting, it also was foreign, peculiar, and a little too "woo-woo" for my mindset at the time. The exotic words she used were hard to remember. My brain did not fully register the notion that yoga had far more to offer than exercise.

What I have since discovered is that the Eight Limbs of Yoga contain a potent philosophy that can have a positive influence on every aspect of your life, especially the way you work. Continuing your on-the-mat practice by living yogic principles off the mat at work will help you become more successful. It will enhance your sense of meaning and purpose in a way that makes work more satisfying and rewarding and less stressful.

The *Bhagavad Gita*, an epic yogic scripture that chronicles conversations between the warrior Arjuna and his spiritual guide, Krishna, emphasizes the importance of work. As Arjuna prepares for battle, Krishna tells him ". . . no one can gain perfection by abstaining from work." He instructs his protégé to attend to his duties, saying, "Perform work in this world, Arjuna, as a man established within himself—without selfish attachments and alike in success and defeat."

Work as yoga was underscored in an email I received from a professor at Fielding Graduate University, where I earned my master's degree. Dr. Barclay Hudson is a yogi, teacher, mentor, and friend. In the context of a class called "Good Work, Meaningful Work," he shared this thought: "It's easy to forget what yoga offers as part of work. We think and talk about 'work–life balance' as if work were something different from life, and different from being alive and conscious."

Jamie and I present yoga practice as both a literal and metaphorical guide to a way of working that can inspire and transform the ways you view what you do to earn a living and how you do it.

GOING OUT ON THE LIMBS

Few people are familiar with the First and Second Limbs of yoga, which concern universal morality (the *yamas*) and outline a personal code of conduct (the *niyamas*). The most well known is the Third Limb, or *asana*, comprised of physical movements meant to prepare the body for meditation. In *asana* classes, most teachers also talk about the importance of breathing, or *pranayama*—this is the Fourth Limb. And the resting pose (*savasana*) that concludes most *asana* practices is a facet of the Fifth Limb, withdrawal of the senses, or *pratyahara*. The Sixth Limb, a practice of focused attention (*dharana*), is somewhat obscure to most practitioners, although many practices incorporate meditation, or *dhyana*, which is the Seventh Limb.

The Eighth Limb is about absorption, unity with the divine, or enlightenment, and is called *samadhi*. It is often seen as an esoteric concept with little practical application in the real world. (That is not our view, as you will see.)

The first two limbs are instructive about forming intentions, making choices about action, and understanding consequences. The remaining limbs speak more to aspects of your mind, which can be trained and shaped through physical movement, breathing, introspection, focus, and meditation. Practitioners gain self-discovery, wisdom, and pragmatic applications to work. With dedication, this leads to absorption or fulfillment, which we define in a practical way for this book: It is cultivating deep understanding of Self. It means consistently aligning your intentions and actions with your highest, most noble purpose, developing your full potential, and recognizing a universal spiritual connection that unites you with something greater than Self.

The Yoga Sutras are brilliantly simple. They are not an attempt to corral or control behavior. They don't delineate "right and wrong," but they do emphasize the role consequences play in any decision. Certain actions reap certain results. Eknath Easwaran, in his introduction to his translation of the *Bhagavad Gita*, calls this the true meaning of *karma*: "Something that is done."

"The law of karma states simply that every act or thought has consequences, which themselves will have consequences. . . . *We ourselves are responsible for what happens to us* [emphasis added], whether or not we can understand how," Easwaran writes. This echoes the message we consistently deliver in our organizational work—you are constantly making choices about how you respond to your circumstances. It's not about whether your choice is definitively right or wrong, or judged good or bad. Knowing that everything has consequences, even your thoughts, is what's important. Yoga's Eight Limbs give you the means to get clear about intentions, the way you see other people and interpret events, your attitudes and actions—and all these things will shape your destiny.

We'll begin this journey with the first two limbs of yoga, each of which has five associated precepts. The First Limb, the *yamas*, contains the precepts of universal morality, also referred to as moral restraints. These suggest a path for creating a world that puts the well-being of all people (indeed, all sentient beings) at the center of every decision you make. If attended to, the *yamas* purify human nature and contribute to the health and happiness of society. Practiced at work, these actions will develop self-awareness and ethical focus, facilitate compassion and collaboration, and foster an orientation that emphasizes personal accountability that sets aside pure self-interest and connects to the whole.

Yoga is a robust and active way of living. The Second Limb, the *niyamas*, provides a guide for helping you develop the capacity to choose "right action" in your daily life. The five precepts that comprise the *niyamas* are more personal, intimate, and call for conscious commitment to apply mindful skill in the art of action.

Lived out, the *yamas* and *niyamas* of yoga will have a significant impact on how you find success—and keep your sanity—in today's chaotic, competitive, and stressful work environments. They are touchstones to return to when your work becomes overwhelming or you find yourself in situations where clarity around right action is murky.

EACH LIMB REINFORCES THE OTHER

Like hands, the *yamas* and *niyamas* each have five fingers, or precepts. Integrated, they create a synergistic strength and energy, just as using ten fingers allows you to accomplish what you could not with one or two. Contained in the clasp of these ten fingers is an inherent compass that can help you stay on a course of ethical, mindful living no matter where your work journey takes you.

The Third Limb, *asana*, is designed to keep the "instrument" of your work—your physical body—in tune. *Asana* has a positive effect on overall health, energy, and well-being, which allows you to better perform your work and successfully serve your enterprise. It also can be an instructive metaphor for the qualities needed to be successful at work: focus, flexibility grounded in stability, balance, and continual improvement (practice!),

Harnessing and controlling the breath, *pranayama*, is the Fourth Limb. It offers techniques for maintaining calm, increasing energy, and keeping you grounded in the most stressful of work environments. Bringing conscious breathing into your work also creates space for clarity and mindful action.

The Fifth Limb, *pratyahara*, is withdrawal of the senses. The root of this term, *ahara*, means "nourishment" and is a practice of examining sensual habits (sometimes referred to as cravings) and the results they have on our actions. *Pratyahara* practice can help you disconnect from a situation to keep instinctual reactions at bay. It develops the skill of being a participant in a situation while simultaneously observing your emotional responses.

The last three limbs represent the results of the actions and practice of the first five limbs. Intense focus, *dharana*, is the Sixth Limb. This practice is training for the mind and helps foster inner awareness of your relationship to surroundings. It further develops your ability to become the "observer," which is useful in all kinds of ways when you're working with others, particularly around issues of communication and accountability.

Meditation is covered by the Seventh Limb, or *dhyana*. A calm, clear mind contributes greatly to work success, as do introspection, self-awareness, and the ability to neutrally observe yourself and others when you're engaged in work. Meditation is training the mind in much the same way you physically train the body. It is key to developing self-awareness. The skill of becoming "the witness" to your emotions and reactions is more finely honed with practice, which fosters your ability to make mindful choices that connect actions to consequences.

The Eighth Limb centers on union with the divine, or *samadhi*, also referred to as absorption or enlightenment. The word means "to bring together, to merge" by bringing everyday actions in line with your supreme self. The practice asks you to recognize and celebrate a force larger than yourself, however you define it, which guides and directs the course of our lives. We will be using work as a metaphor for recognizing your purpose and potential, helping others develop theirs, and using your energies to create an enlightened workplace that serves everyone.

SUGGESTIONS ON HOW TO USE THIS BOOK

It is not necessary to read this book in sequence to understand the precepts, but it is important to understand that each limb builds upon and strengthens the others. Many of them overlap. In most cases, it is not possible to violate one without violating others.

We'll be sharing the stories of people who have used these precepts to help them be more effective, satisfied, and sane at work. We hope this will breathe life into the ways you can practice the eight limbs, and help you consider how the precepts might apply to your own work life. At the end of each chapter, reflective questions or suggestions are offered to help you set intentions and create a personal guide for mindful work practices. These are not intended to be homework assignments, nor do we think you need to tackle them one by one. Select the ones that resonate for you—or ignore them completely!

Yoga is a journey and a lifelong practice. Trying to take in everything at once might feel overwhelming or exhausting. We suggest you luxuriate in the limbs, as you would a warm bath. If a thought or concept resonates or seems worth thinking about, consider flagging it with a sticky note or some other marker so you can return to it. Remember, there are no commands in yoga. Our suggestions are intended to provide a frame for thinking about the way you currently operate at work and what might be different if you began a mindful practice in that context. You could consider doing one exercise a week or one a month. Or if you're not ready for action, perhaps it would be useful to do a sitting meditation on something that calls to you.

The journey is yours. We have intended to write a guidebook with suggestions for making it more rich and satisfying.

two

THE FIRST LIMB:
UNIVERSAL MORALITY

~~~~~~

We are here to awake from
our illusion of separateness.

Thich Nhat Hanh

~~~~~~

THE *YAMAS*

Most religions or philosophies speak to some aspect of the morality contained in the words of the Sutra referencing the *yamas*. Robert Johnson's classic treatise on Patanjali's Sutras explains that "The commandments [*yamas*] form the broad general training of humanity. Each rests on a universal spiritual law." Patanjali says that the commandments are not limited to any "race, place, time, or occasion." They are to be integrated into daily living.

Often called the moral restraints, the precepts in the *yamas* are universal, and are framed as the "do nots" in life's list of moral do's and don'ts. The precepts contained within this First Limb are:

Ahimsa—non-violence

Satya—non-lying

Asteya—non-stealing

Brahmacharya—non-squandering of vital energies

Aparigraha—non-greed, non-hoarding

Put into positive wording, *ahimsa* asks that you eschew all forms of violence and treat all living things with respect and compassion. *Satya* is a commitment to truthfulness and transparency. *Asteya* means we take only that which is freely given. *Brahmacharya* is about controlling our senses and energies so we can cultivate our inner life, and *aparigraha* is about living simply by taking or using nothing more than what we truly need.

Let's explore the precepts through the lens of your work.

NON-VIOLENCE
(Ahimsa)

Compassion, loving kindness

~~~~~~

Non-violence leads to the highest ethics, which is the goal of all evolution. Until we stop harming all other living things, we are still savages.

Thomas Edison

~~~~~~

I practiced Bikram yoga for about three years in the early 2000s, in a little studio in downtown Hollywood, Florida. Bikram Choudhury created this practice in India and imported it to the United States in the 1970s. It consists of 26 poses, always done in the same order, performed in rooms that are heated to 100 degrees or more.

The teachers, Ron and Nancy, would always start class with questions and cautions: "Is this the first time for anyone? Are there health issues we should be aware of?"

In one class, a middle-aged man with glasses raised his hand when Ron asked about first-timers. He received Ron's customary warning to take it slow and easy. The heat could be debilitating, and it was important to listen when the body said "Whoa!" As usual, Ron reminded people to drink plenty of water, and if they became overheated or dizzy, to immediately drop into a resting pose until they felt ready to rejoin the class. The middle-aged first-timer assured Ron that he was an athlete and very fit. Not to worry, he could do it.

The student proceeded to do the poses with vigor, ignoring Ron's occasional suggestions that perhaps he should back off a bit. About thirty minutes into the class, the be-spectacled student pitched face forward in a faint. His glasses cracked and blood gushed from a cut on his forehead. Class was suspended as Ron rushed him to the emergency room.

❧

Non-violence, the first precept in the *yamas*, is founda-tional. One who is committed to *ahimsa* would find it al-most impossible to violate any of the others.

It might seem obvious, and easy to live: Do Not Kill. Do Not Injure. Do Not Harm. Most of us don't intend to do those things in the course of our work days, so how hard could practicing *ahimsa* really be?

But violence, harm, and injury have incarnations that do not always appear so overt or obvious, especially in the workplace. More importantly, people are sometimes imper-vious to the harm they do to themselves. Just like the man whose ego drove him to go too far in the Bikram class, so can pushing yourself too hard at work result in injury, pain, and lost opportunities.

A place to start opening your eyes to *ahimsa* is by mak-ing visible the ways you unconsciously do "violence" to yourself.

Think about your work habits. How long do you sit at your desk before you get up to walk, stretch, and take healthy nourishment—refreshing yourself with mental and physical breaks? Do you maintain a schedule that extends your days long beyond the time you have energy and focus, leaving you exhausted and depleted? These habits can be harmful to your physical, mental, and emotional self, and in the end, make you less effective. Instead of pushing yourself to exhaustion, consider how much better you can serve yourself and those around you when you are well-nourished, well-rested, and energized.

SELF-TO-SELF CONVERSATIONS

How do you talk to yourself throughout the day? Do you let your inner critic go wild with messages that batter your esteem or make you feel less than worthy? Do you allow the harsh words of others to take you to a place of self-blame, anger, defensiveness, or depression?

Pandit Rajmani Tigunait was ordained into the 5,000-year-old lineage of the Himalayan masters by Swami Rama. He is the spiritual head of the Himalayan Institute in Honesdale, Pennsylvania, and has written about how negative self-talk is a form of violence: "No one is closer to you than yourself. Stop hurting yourself by telling yourself that you are a failure. By judging and condemning yourself, you are dishonoring the greatest gift that providence has given you."

Listening—worse yet, believing—the chatter of your inner critic only conjures dark clouds of doubt and fear that block your internal light. Doubting that you are worthy inhibits development of your full potential. You are worthy, as worthy as anyone, no matter what your job, your title, or your rank. If you make a mistake, so what? It's not going to get undone by beating yourself up. Acknowledge what happened, apologize to those you hurt, and forgive yourself. Reflect on what can be learned from the incident, and let it go. Staying stuck in self-recrimination doesn't serve anyone.

To paraphrase Gandhi, change means becoming that which you want to see in the world, so being forgiving and compassionate to yourself is the initial and essential cornerstone to practicing *ahimsa* out in the world.

Kallie teaches yoga at a military university in Vermont and also earns a living as a freelance writer. The latter occupation, she says, "comes with an overwhelming amount of built-in rejection. That kind of rejection can really feel like a blow if I let it."

She has written a play that is in development, in which she also has an acting and singing role. Rehearsal one day was in a downward spiral—she and a fellow actor had not managed to strike the right tone. The director, cast, and crew were frustrated. After blowing a song with her costar, she started laughing to release the tension. As her partner stormed off the stage, her stomach clenched as the acid of self-doubt set in. She credits her longtime yoga practice with helping her keep it in perspective.

"As he stomped off, I was just watching myself withering down, feeling horrible about myself, all the insecurities rushing to the surface. And then I had this insight, which was directly tied to my yoga practice," Kallie says. "I realized it doesn't matter if this project is a failure or a success. If it doesn't work out, it won't mean I don't have talent or that I am a bad person."

Yoga helps her with mastery of the ego, Kallie says. It reminds her that attachment to an outcome leads to misery, so when editors decline an article or her book project stalls for lack of a publisher, she doesn't take it personally. Self-blame is counterproductive.

Developing the ability to internalize compassion and forgiveness for yourself makes it much easier to extend that to others in a way that practices *ahimsa* in its broadest application.

LEARNING TO SEE THE "INVISIBLE"

Using a wide lens of non-violence (*ahimsa*), consider how you treat others at work. Like most people, you are probably polite and friendly toward your coworkers. It's unlikely you consciously look for ways to hurt others. But look a little closer. Small, subtle acts of violence are accepted in many work cultures: gossip, manipulation, lack of compassion and respect. When such acts are commonly practiced and accepted, they have the potential to become invisible. It's easy to become blind to the fact that seemingly minor deeds inflict real damage and injury.

How do you treat colleagues when the stakes are high and things are not going so well? When you are angry, do you blow up, or cut others down with sarcasm or unkind humor? Have you ignored people you don't like, refusing them the courtesy of a "Good morning!" or "How are you today?" Have you found ways to exclude people you don't like or consider difficult to work with from important conversations or meetings? Do you shut down people who don't see things the way you do?

Here is a tough question: how often do you talk about people when they're not in the room? Malicious gossip might seem like an obvious violation of *ahimsa*, but critiquing someone's performance when they are not in the room, or making decisions about job assignments and work roles without their participation, also can be a form of violence. These common work practices come with a likelihood of creating hurt feelings, misunderstandings, and injury to someone's reputation or standing. It also decelerates development of their potential and inhibits the best possible work results. People know that their livelihood and their opportunities can be affected by the work assignments they receive and the content of their performance reviews. Involving people in conversations about the decisions that have a great impact on their lives is a way of practicing *ahimsa* at work.

If you are in a position to influence the actions or work practices of others, how do you do it in a way that keeps non-injury or non-harm at the forefront of your actions? Supervisors, managers, and leaders have been entrusted with a kind of power to "get things done." Wielding that power in a way that abuses others, even in the name of achievement or accomplishment, is a form of violence. When wielding a title or a position of authority becomes a method of getting your way, even if done through something as innocuous as name-dropping, it will create a climate of fear and resentment that is a disservice to you, those with whom you interact, and the work you're all there to do.

Threats, attempts to manipulate or to rule over others, are harmful, an attempt to subdue freedom and self-determination by asserting control. In addition, such actions damage the enterprise because people take actions to please the boss in order to get ahead, rather than considering how to best serve customers and other stakeholders for the good of the business.

Practicing *ahimsa* will help you increase your awareness of these harmful acts and develop strategies for eliminating them. You can inoculate yourself to the negative effects they have on you and others. Lawrence, a non-commissioned officer in the U.S. Army, started practicing yoga a few years ago on a dare while living in Vermont. Now stationed in a combat zone, he says yoga helps him remain calm, allowing him to focus on the safety and well-being of his team on base, as well as in violent, volatile environments.

"I am known to have a short fuse," Lawrence says. "But yoga has helped me curb my temper and control my emotions. Obviously, a war zone is not the best place to let emotions cloud your judgment."

SPEAK UP! WELL-BEING BEFORE PROFITS

When people choose to put profits ahead of the safety and well-being of their fellow humans, *ahimsa* is violated. Think about the outcome of the housing industry collapse of 2008—where mortgage and investment bankers were obsessed with making money from their investments instead of best serving their customers. Their risky practices culminated in a form of violence—recession, unemployment, and people losing their homes. How many people lost their homes when they knowingly took out loans they knew they could not afford? How different things would have been if all these decision-makers were fully committed to living the precept of *ahimsa*?

And just because you don't have the authority of a CEO or senior manager, you are not powerless. Individual actions can be powerful, and they matter. When you see an unsafe, risky, or morally wrong situation and choose to ignore it, you could be unwittingly responsible for future violence. The Penn State scandal, involving an assistant football coach who was molesting young boys, is a heartbreaking example. Numerous people, including those who were in the highest echelons of the organization, were aware of the coach's inappropriate and abusive actions, but failed to report it immediately or swept allegations aside to protect the university's image. A culture of power, arrogance, and fear conspired to protect the institution rather than the boys.

Examples of workplace *ahimsa* violations, where people could have spoken up about dangerous or unethical conditions but didn't, are depressingly plentiful. For example, safety violations were cited in three major mining disasters that occurred in West Virginia from 2006 to 2010, which took 43 lives. The BP oil spill in the Gulf of Mexico—a tragedy that cost lives, livelihoods, and horrific damage to the environment—could have been averted if the well-being of employees, rather than shareholder profits, had been at the forefront of decision-making.

Raising your consciousness about working conditions, how work practices affect the environment, then doing what you can to make improvements, is a yogic practice that serves you, your coworkers, and the workplace.

THE BLAME GAME AND BEYOND

Blame can be another subtle way to violate *ahimsa*. Anandaroopa, who worked for a multinational bank in Asia, was frightened and horrified when his boss blamed him for a situation over which he had no control. The bank was being investigated for tax evasion in a communist country, and most of the employees chalked it up to politics. But they were uneasy as it became clear their actions were being closely monitored, and people were being called in for "interviews" by the communist authorities. "In this country, people don't have the same rights as they do in the U.S.," Anandaroopa says. "The authorities could haul people in for questioning at any time and detain them for up to a year. It was a really tense time."

When Anandaroopa was brought in for questioning, authorities showed him signed statements from the bank's president. The statements alleged that Anandaroopa was the mastermind behind any tax irregularities. "I was stunned and scared. I was close to both [the bank president] and his wife. It definitely felt like they had committed an act of violence against me." Although the bank was eventually cleared, the parent company's officials felt it was too risky to do business in that country and decided to shut the bank down. And the bank president assigned Anandaroopa, the assistant he had blamed for tax irregularities, the job of firing people.

The suffering Anandaroopa endured from traumatic experiences at the bank led him back to yoga, which he had flirted with briefly as a college student. Now his story serves as a cautionary tale of how easy it is to inflict violence at work by mindlessly following instructions. Although his boss knew people were going to lose their jobs, he protected himself instead of showing compassion, kindness, and regard for workers' dignity.

CREATING SPACE FOR COMPASSION

Kindness and compassion are the flip side of violence. If you can't muster these in a heated moment, developing strategies and skills that give you space to regain your composure will help you move away from negative action and toward *ahimsa*.

Thomas, who works with people who have disabilities, says his yoga practice helps him keep *ahimsa* in mind when things begin to unravel. He supports a man who relies on others to help him bathe, dress, cook, eat, and get to work. His physical and emotional disabilities are a source of great frustration, which leads to blow-ups. For Thomas, it can create a volatile and stressful work environment.

Practicing *ahimsa* has been key to helping Thomas stay calm and compassionate in the face of emotional outbursts and helps him remember it is not personal when his client lashes out. *Ahimsa* helps keep the relationship functional—Thomas has learned to step away from a situation that is getting too heated or out of control.

"Yoga allows me to be of better service," Thomas says. "I do best when I have compassion for what he is going through, and *ahimsa* also tells me when to remove myself from a situation where I am tempted to do or say something unkind." He knows they both will benefit from time and space to calm down. He tells his client it is time for a break, and steps out of the room to refocus on what he is there to do—be of service.

AHIMSA IN A VIOLENT WORLD

Lacey, a police officer who teaches yoga in her off-duty hours, sees both of her jobs as contributing to a less violent world. She is a sergeant on the police force in Las Vegas, a town rife with all the temptations appealing to human nature's basest instincts. She says yoga literally has saved her life (more in Chapter Five) and her sanity. "The stress of being a cop will drive you over the edge. I've seen other cops deal with it through pain pills, alcohol, girls, gambling . . . you name it. Yoga is what I do instead. It keeps me clearheaded."

She sees the irony of trying to practice *ahimsa* in a job that sometimes requires her to use violent means to stop people who intend to hurt others. Lacey was initially shattered when she experienced a police officer's worst possible scenario: taking the life of a human being in order to protect others. "That was really hard on me. I take *ahimsa* seriously, and I really struggled. After it happened, I called my teacher to talk it through. He told me that for the warrior, violence is always a last resort Even so, the warrior also has to stand ready. If drastic actions are necessary to protect yourself and the community—and if those actions ultimately save lives—then that is practicing *ahimsa*. If we are doing our job right, and our presence helps decrease crime, that is *ahimsa*. As police officers, we try to stop others from doing harm by using the least force possible. That is *ahimsa*."

Five suggestions for practicing ahimsa

1. Commit to a day of noticing your internal conversations. Journal about it at the end of the day and see what you discover. Do you need to change the conversation?

2. Make a list of the short- and long-term consequences for you, your coworkers, and the business when you push yourself too aggressively, or ask others to do the same. How does *ahimsa* apply in those situations?

3. Who are the people you know or admire that exemplify *ahimsa* in their work? List the ways you see them doing this. How might you adopt similar actions?

4. Make a list of the gains that come with practicing *ahimsa*, as well as the potential losses. What would you have to give up in order to gain the benefits of *ahimsa*? Remember that all gains are not positive, and all losses are not negative. For instance, you might gain a fear of being seen as weak or ineffective, or lose the ability to wield your power the way you have been accustomed to.

5. Create intentions around a practice of non-violence. Make a list of the ways you could integrate this practice into your work. What one thing can you commit to do for a day, a week, or a month that would expand your on-the-job practice of this precept?

NON-LYING
(Satya)
Commitment to truth

~~~~~~

*There are only two mistakes one can make
along the road to truth—not going all the way,
and not starting.*

Buddha

~~~~~~

While working in California in the early days of our relationship, Jamie and I decided to attend a Bikram class together. Jamie had never done that type of yoga and wanted
to have the experience. We moved through the series of
poses as a young, lithe, and driven teacher gave instructions, occasionally demonstrating and making corrections.

When it was time to do reclining hero pose (*supta
virasana*), I shot Jamie a worried look. The pose entails sitting on your legs, seat between feet, while working your
torso back to lie on the floor. Jamie suffered a high school
football injury that resulted in major surgery, so it's impossible for him to bend his right knee much past 90 degrees.
"You might want to skip this one," I whispered. But he attempted it as best he could.

The instructor marched over, plopped herself next to
Jamie's mat, and expertly dropped into a flawless pose.
"Come on," she said to him, loudly enough for everyone
to hear. "What's this? I have an 80-year-old student who
can do this pose better than you are!"

During my first course of teacher training, a class discussion on "right speech" included four questions to consider each time you speak. The questions resonated because they aligned so perfectly with the principles of the *Authentic Conversations* workshops I was learning to teach inside organizations. I could see how the questions, if answered positively, would instantly elevate conversations into a more authentic realm.

1. Is it true?

2. Is it necessary?

3. Is it kind?

4. Does it improve upon the silence?

(We have also seen these questions incorporated into the acronym THINK: True, Helpful, Improves upon the silence, Necessary, Kind.)

Was the Bikram yoga teacher's comment to Jamie true? We have neither reason nor evidence to believe she didn't know an 80-year-old woman who could do reclining hero pose. But was the comment necessary, helpful, or kind? Did it improve upon the silence?

THE THREE ELEMENTS OF TRUTH

It is no coincidence that the first question is about truth. That is the standard of *satya*, the second *yama*. We see truth as having three facets:

1. Telling the truth as you know it

2. Being willing to hear another's truth as they know it

3. Understanding that many things can be true at the same time

At work, the third point is an important and often over-looked facet of a truth-telling (*satya*) where versions of "What happened here?" and "Who did what?" are numerous and have significant ramifications. When things get derailed or problems arise, trying to untangle "who said what to whom and when" can create an energy-sapping blame game. In addition, claiming that your experience is the only "truth" is the antithesis of learning. The lessons of discovery that spring from understanding multiple points of view, each of which is experienced as true for the individual, get lost in defensiveness and recrimination.

Truth—in terms of honesty, transparency, engagement, and respect—can be a rare commodity in the work world. Knowledge is often seen as power, manipulation is widely practiced and considered acceptable, and people are consumed with covering their bacon. Even so, it would be hard to argue that practicing *satya* is not essential for a truly successful enterprise. It creates the necessary conditions for work cultures that operate based on:

~ People trusting each other

~ Knowledge and understanding

~ Connection to others

~ Confidence in the enterprise

~ Commitment to a vision

The number of people in organizations who complain to us that they can't possibly tell the truth at work is striking and disheartening. People see being honest as a radical act. It is too risky, a possible career killer. They report that telling their truth has resulted in negative repercussions at work. They insist it's not safe to do so, and tell us stories to back it up. "Management (my coworker, my boss, the customer) doesn't want to hear the truth" is a common refrain. And when they say this, we understand they are speaking their truth. No doubt about it—it takes great courage to tell the truth with goodwill, especially when the culture doesn't support honesty or candor. Even so, it might be worth examining how much of the risk is real or perceived—what direct evidence or data do you have that speaking up for the good of the business would put your job at risk? Here is another important question: what is the cost to you and the business when you're living in an environment that no one can believe in?

SATYA IS THE FOUNDATION OF TRUST

On the flip side, it is not uncommon to hear CEOs and senior managers we work with say they can't be transparent about the workings of the business because "those people can't handle it." The truth just worries people unnecessarily, they say. It creates a distraction and raises too many questions that are not easy to answer. In our view, such statements are about leaders trying to be responsible for someone else's emotional reactions—which is impossible. And what is likely at play is a fear of having to deal with others' emotional reactions. We are not the only ones who hear these stories. Our colleagues who do similar work share similar experiences.

Lying is a horrible business practice, no matter what your intentions. Hundreds of books have been written, many of them based on respected research, citing the marketplace advantages of ethical and transparent business practices in creating successful, sustainable businesses. People *can* handle the truth. Consider the times at work you felt lied to. Is that a better feeling than having to face a harsh business reality? Organizations often spend hundreds of thousands of dollars on consultants, training, and designing policies aimed at building trust in the workplace. A committed *satya* practice would create the same thing with little cost and great efficiency.

ELIMINATING THE SPIN CYCLE

Truth-telling, or *satya*, is among five core ethical values found in almost every culture in the world, according to research done by the Institute for Global Ethics. IGE has surveyed hundreds of thousands of people in diverse cultures around the world, seeking to understand the core values that constitute cultural morality. Truth-telling and honesty always rise to the top, along with respect, justice, responsibility, and compassion.

And yet *satya* is often seen as something that can be, even should be, set aside in the cause of protecting the image of a business or institution, even if it harms employees, customers, and other stakeholders. Consider this common scenario: A meeting or press conference is convened to announce that a high profile and formerly powerful person is resigning to "spend time with family" or is leaving to "pursue [undisclosed] opportunities." That kind of announcement is so common that it has become a joke, a wink-wink admission that we all know what really is going on. Salvaging an ego, upholding an image, and keeping the dirty laundry hidden away is more important than telling the truth and building trust. Not only are lies told, people also are in the dark about what is really going on, creating fear and uncertainty.

When Carol Bartz, a former CEO at Yahoo, was fired, she took immediate control of the message rather than waiting for a corporate communication specialist to come up with the spin. She did something executives rarely do in that situation—quickly sent out a companywide email alerting people she had been let go:

To all: I am very sad to tell you that I've just been fired over the phone by Yahoo's Chairman of the Board. It has been my pleasure to work with all of you and I wish you only the best going forward. Carol

As word of her action got out, reactions were varied: Was this a bold act of authenticity and transparency? Or was it reckless, spiteful, and harmful to Yahoo's image? Bartz's defenders said her action was consistent with her direct management style, and many applauded her refreshing honesty. They expressed hope that such candor would become a trend. Regardless of how you view her action, the fact it generated so much controversy is a telling commentary on the kinds of workplace cultures that have been created by setting aside *satya*. Had Bartz allowed the company to deliver the traditional "left to pursue other opportunities" message, people could discern the lie, which contributes to lack of trust, which creates a world that no one really believes in.

While this honesty is most definitely a moral issue, it also has pragmatic aspects at work. What are the costs to businesses when you see telling the truth as a radical or risky act? You build a culture with an implicit rule that critical thinking, creativity, and collaboration are not valued. How can you or the enterprise where you work achieve full potential when protecting egos or demanding obedience supersedes building trust? How can innovation, creativity, diversity of thought, and collective wisdom serve the enterprise when you are afraid to speak your truth? Or refuse to hear the truth of others? How can people commit to fully serving the workplace if they don't understand how and why decisions are made?

Manipulating others at work is commonly practiced, to the point that it is often seen as an acceptable "best practice" for getting ahead. In *Authentic Conversations*, we define manipulation as trying to get someone to do something you want them to do without revealing your real intentions. This is impossible to do without a form of lying, because you're withholding a complete picture. You are saying, "Getting the outcome I want is more important to me than honoring your right to make decisions based on full knowledge."

Imagine a workplace where you and everyone you know are committed to *satya*. What changes?

THE "HOW" OF *SATYA*

The third question, "Is it kind?," should be considered every time you decide it is necessary to speak your truth. Brutal honesty rarely serves, and won't be heard as well as a message delivered with goodwill and compassion. A phenomenon that sometimes occurs in our organizational work is that people hear "authentic conversations" and make the erroneous translation of "brutal honesty." It's a false and counterproductive equivalency. As T. K. V. Desikachar points out in *The Heart of Yoga*, "Satya should never come into conflict with our efforts to behave with *ahimsa* (non-violence)." Goodwill doesn't require anything more than making a choice about who you want to be when you bring yourself to a conversation. *Satya* means communicating with kindness even if you haven't been able to muster warm and fuzzy feelings toward the person you are addressing.

Kimberly, who teaches yoga part-time and works full-time as a food server in a popular bistro in Phoenix, credits her yoga practice with creating a more productive relationship with her manager. After receiving several harsh text messages from him criticizing her work, she was feeling attacked, defensive, and resentful. In spite of his reluctance to talk about the issue directly, she insisted they sit down for a face-to-face conversation, hoping he would be willing to hear her truth. But she also realized it was important to be honest with herself. "I knew I had to go inward first. I had to shift my perspective from defensiveness to a consideration of what I had been doing to contribute to the difficult situation."

In the conversation with her manager, she explained what was going on for her, and asked him to explain what was going on for him. He brought up two difficult issues, one of which she owned. As for the other, she explained why she had done what she did. Kimberly says, "Yoga helped me be conscious of not wanting to stay stuck in resentment and create a situation where I was miserable at work. I wouldn't be doing my best in that situation. The conversation ended up being super productive. [My manager] can come off as mean sometimes, but in that conversation he wasn't. I was glad I did not let these issues just go into the abyss."

One of the great lessons I took from several years of newspaper reporting is that "two sides to a story" is a myth—

there are infinite sides. As Oscar Wilde said, "The truth is rarely pure and never simple." When someone is sincere and honest in expressing the truth of her experience, that version of the story is "true." Acknowledging that many things can be true at the same time enhances your ability to truly hear others, be curious about their point of view, and find common understanding that serves the whole.

SILENCE AS A VIOLATION OF SATYA

Keeping quiet when work could be more successful with your input is a form of dishonoring truth. For example, if you stay quiet about your doubts and reservations in a meeting when decisions are being made, it is a form of withholding truth. Trashing the decision afterward in "the meeting after the meeting" is another violation, because you appeared to be going along with a decision you have questions about or don't intend to support. Fear might keep you from speaking up when you see a problem that others don't. Who wants to be seen as a naysayer? However, speaking up with the intention of helping, when done with goodwill and without attachment to getting your way, will better serve the business. And if you can't muster up the courage to speak your truth, trashing the decision afterward chips away at your integrity.

Depending on your workplace, negative consequences may be attached for speaking your mind. But what consequences are attached to your integrity and to decision-making when you don't? And how much of your reluctance springs from willingness to own and be accountable for your truth? Non-lying is much more than knowingly stating a falsehood. *Satya* also asks you to be forthright, transparent, and ethical in your communication. Its corollary is developing a willingness to listen to the truth of others. If you have knowledge that others need to make a more informed decision, or reservations based on things you believe to be true, the silence *will* be improved if you offer that up. It doesn't mean your viewpoint always prevails, but it fosters trust and improves the quality of decision-making.

Staying silent can also be tempting in the face of having to own up to your mistakes or admit your contribution to a difficult circumstance. By cultivating a *satya* practice, you can do these things knowing you are engaging others with transparency and building relationships everyone can believe in. Truth-telling in this situation also sends a powerful message about personal accountability, signals a willingness to take risks, and creates an opportunity for learning.

Trying to see others' perspectives is an important part of Kimberly's *satya* practice, she says. "Even in a situation where I don't really think I have contributed to a problem, I at least try and put myself in their position so I can figure out what they think my contribution might be. And that usually leads me to realize I really did have a hand in creating the problem."

Being mindful about the ways we label and judge others can help us with another subtle form of violating *satya*—projecting our judgments onto others and seeing them as "truth." Judith Hanson Lasater, a master yoga teacher based in California, writes about this in *What We Say Matters*, which she co-authored with her husband, lawyer Ike K. Lasater. "One of the surest ways to disconnect from ourselves and temporarily forget the values of *satya* . . . is to project enemy images onto other people or even onto ourselves." It's distressingly easy to tell yourself stories about who you think you see. How often do you see people cast others as enemies, or give them labels such as "lazy" or "suck-ups" or "stupid"? When you create stories about others' motivations and actions, fabricating elaborate scenarios that you can't possibly know are true, it violates *satya*. My yoga practice has made me aware of how often I do this, and it's a tough habit to break.

Improving upon the silence sets a high standard for communication. But just pausing to ask the question is a worthwhile effort. At the very least, it gives you space to reflect upon what you will be saying and consider the effect it could have on others.

~~~~~

Five suggestions for practicing satya

1. Make a list of the ways *satya* could improve the results of your work, your unit's work, or the company's effectiveness.

2. Commit to a day at work where you make a note every time you violate *satya*. Did you stay silent in a meeting when you should have spoken up? Give someone a false compliment? Give a partial explanation to a story to cast yourself in a better light? Without judgment, journal about the motivation behind these actions. What is so compelling about doing this?

3. List some of the ways you honor *satya*. Then list reasons you violate the precept. What are the triggers in both situations? What are you trying to avoid or gain?

4. When you listen to others at work talk, especially if you disagree with them, ask yourself, "What is true about

what he or she is saying?" What changes as you look for the answer? How do you express your point of view with goodwill?

5. Commit to a day at work when you ask the four questions before you speak: "True? Necessary? Kind? Improves upon the silence?" How did it change the quality of your interactions?

NON-STEALING
(Asteya)

Taking only that which is freely given

~~~~~~

The desire to possess and enjoy what another has, drives a person to do evil . . . not only taking what belongs to another without permission, but also using something for a different purpose to that intended or beyond the time permitted by its owner.

BKS Iyengar

~~~~~~

Sara was almost always the last to arrive to yoga class. On her best days, she would barely manage to unroll her mat before the teacher began centering the class. One day, she glanced around the room, observing the others who had arrived early. They looked peaceful and grounded as they sat quietly, eyes closed, ready to drop inward. She was still breathing heavily and distracted.

As a career coach, author, and in-demand speaker, Sara was constantly trying to stuff ten pounds of her life into a five-pound container of time. Consequently, she typically arrived at her appointments late, harried, and distracted. She knew it was rude. She wanted to change. And yet she continually yielded to the habit.

Her yoga practice was a refuge from the crazed internal metronome that drove her through the day, and she was grateful to have a place to unplug. As she found herself envying her fellow practitioners' serenity that day, Sara wondered, "Why don't I do that?"

It struck her: Chronic tardiness is stealing. When she arrived late, she stole others' time and cheated herself out of peace. Sara silently committed to arriving to yoga early so she had time to disconnect before class began and receive the full benefit of the practice. As she honored that commitment, the new habit began spilling over into the rest of her life.

❧

Non-stealing (*asteya*) asks us to take only that which is freely given. You don't have to be an embezzler or pocket merchandise from the warehouse to be a thief, although many people find ways to rationalize that. We have one friend who worked as a bookkeeper for a highly regarded consultant who worked with clients throughout the world. He would arrange two or three engagements in the same area, and then bill all of them for airfare, raking in two or three times the amount he was justifiably owed. When our friend objected to the practice, the consultant told her not to worry about it. "They would have had to pay my airfare if I wasn't seeing those other clients, so it's a legitimate way of billing," he told her. "And it's too confusing to divide it up among three clients."

It might seem harmless when you walk off with small things such as office supplies or postage, or use the company copy machine for personal business, but it violates *asteya* and has an impact on the financial health of the enterprise where you work. One yogini told us that during her student days, she worked at a restaurant where soda refills for customers were a dollar. Many of the employees refilled the soda and pocketed the extra dollar—definitely not living out *asteya*. If you have not been invited to supplement your income that way, it's stealing.

These are some of the traditional ways of thinking about stealing, but this precept calls for more than just avoiding the obvious thefts of money and material things. When you consider the incomparable value of time, energy, self-worth, and reputation, you probably watch some sort of larceny being committed every day. A commitment to *asteya* means being mindful of all the ways you might be taking things that are not given freely.

A corollary to this *yama* is developing the quality of generosity. This is a wonderful way to develop your potential and that of others. *Asteya* keeps you connected to a world that is truly abundant by asking that you take only that which is freely given, and calling on you to be generous with others.

THIEVING WITHOUT THINKING

At work, it's easy to move through the day without realizing how often you are stealing from others that which is impossible to recover. How many times have you heard the sarcastic remark, "That is an hour of my life I never will get back"? Practicing non-stealing (*asteya*) is a way to enhance our awareness of what is valuable, as well as mindfully respect what belongs to others. The practice benefits from a well-developed sense of humility and self-restraint. An unnecessary email, mindlessly interrupting a coworker who is focused on her work, constantly showing up late to meetings—these things take time from others that has not been freely given. Habit is a culprit, because we often do things without first considering the impact it could have on others.

How often do you hit "reply all" to an email before considering how vital the content is to everyone on the distribution list? When a meeting is scheduled for 9 A.M., are you habitually there at 9:05 A.M.? If you show up harried and unprepared, people have to take time to fill you in or decision-making is delayed. It's time theft.

It's a great thing to connect with others and express caring about their lives, but how often do work conversations devolve into kvetching about something or someone at work you dislike? Plopping down in a coworker's workspace to indulge in idle chitchat or dissect the latest rumor going around robs at least two people's time. Could that time be invested more productively, maybe by looking for ways to repair a relationship or resolve a difficult issue? How many meetings are stalled by unnecessary arguments or failures to follow through on previous commitments? Tangential conversations, when they remove your attention from the work to be done, are a big contributor to violating *asteya* at work.

After Diego, an investment banker, developed a committed yoga practice, he started realizing that some of his work practices "stole time" from clients and coworkers. "Stealing money? That's what people think about, and that would be obvious and easy," he says. "But stealing time? Time is all we have. It is the point!"

He decided that he should be as careful with time investments as he was with his clients' financial holdings. These days, Diego schedules meetings only after thinking carefully about the purpose—what needs to get accomplished, and whether the work or decision-making can be done in a more time-efficient way. He develops agendas for attendees beforehand, and encourages others to show up well prepared.

Just before he hits the "send" key, he reviews the email distribution list to ensure everyone truly needs the information. People have begun to notice that Diego's emails are pithy and to the point, which saves them time and aids in understanding. "I realized I had been in the habit of over-informing people, and mindlessly copying a lot of people. Most of the time, it was for my own benefit. When I started looking at unnecessary emails as 'stealing space' from people's inboxes, I stopped filling them up with irrelevant emails."

Donna Farhi, an author and master yoga teacher who has taught for three decades, talks about *asteya* from the viewpoint of self-reliance: "Not stealing demands that we cultivate a certain level of self-sufficiency so that we do not demand more of others, our family, or our community than we need."

At work, becoming self-sufficient also allows you to work efficiently, as well as preventing time theft with unnecessary interruptions. Being self-directed and deeply literate about your workplace allows you to better serve the whole, and makes it easier to collaborate with others on ways to work more efficiently. When you take the initiative to learn about work processes, the interdependencies needed to get work done, and what really matters to the business, it will help more get accomplished in less time.

One common complaint we hear about in organizations is bosses who spend most of their time micromanaging. This could also be a form of stealing, because it robs people of the opportunities for personal development, critical thinking, and independence.

STEALING THE CREDIT

Work practices can conspire to make you an unwitting thief if you're not mindful. When I was a senior manager at a major newspaper, I used to receive an annual bonus for meeting certain companywide goals developed by the senior directors. Looking back, it is clear I was pretty cavalier about recognizing that those goals really got accomplished through the talent and commitment of the hard-working staff I supervised. *Satya* (non-lying) compels me to say that it was a great feeling to get that extra cash at the end of the year. But now I find myself wondering why *everyone* in an organization doesn't get commensurately rewarded with bonuses when goals are met and profits are healthy. Each person who contributes to a healthy bottom line deserves credit and financial reward, from the CEO to the front desk receptionist.

When Jamie worked at a major consulting firm several years ago, he and his late business partner, Joel Henning, were insistent that "bonus equality" become a standard business practice. The year-end bonus pool was divided by the total number of employees and everyone got an equal share. This meant some employees got bonuses that were almost equal to their annual salary. (This also is a practice of *aparigraha*, or non-greed, which we will explore later.)

How often have you watched as others neglected to mention the efforts of all team members when it came time to give credit? Have you done it yourself? Accomplishment is almost always the result of many hands and minds working together. Why would you rob the whole by assigning credit to one or a handful of people? Practicing *asteya* allows everyone to be included and rewarded—and reflects the reality of achievement.

GIVING FREELY

As we talked to people about *asteya* in preparation for writing this book, we got a long list of answers when we asked folks about the ways it could be violated. Resources. Energy. Time. Optimism. Unfair wages. Reputation. One yogi said, "You can demand another's respect or high regard, without even realizing that it is only something of worth when it is freely given." Pondering the ways it is possible to violate *asteya* can be overwhelming, and the opportunities to do so can be obvious or subtle. But getting obsessive about non-stealing is not the point. Awareness is. What can be gained from noticing what is freely given, and what can be taken away without anyone even thinking about it as a theft?

To be sure, everyone is in charge of his or her own time, energy, motivation, and outlook. It is easy to lose sight of the fact that you and everyone you know are making choices about how to manage those things. It is equally easy to cast yourself as a victim when others make off with your time, sap your energy, and rob your peace of mind—even though you ultimately have control over how you deal with such circumstances. Practicing *asteya* will help you see what truly is of worth, be more mindful about using what you have, and honor that which belongs to others.

When Corinne landed a job in a large university after working alone for many years, she began noticing how easily *asteya* could be unwittingly violated. "Before this job, I had mostly worked on my own, and I never realized the chatter that goes on about other people," she says. "I can't say I've never succumbed to it myself, but when I think about this in terms of my yoga practice, I do think it is a violation of *asteya*. We are being paid to do work. Gossiping not only steals time away from work, it also can be a form of stealing people's morale. If I go even deeper, I also feel like we're robbing the person being talked about of their whole self. I have to catch myself and say, 'That's not okay.'"

For a long time, Corinne stayed silent as others chattered around her, because she didn't want to "come off as being too motherly or superior by pointing out what is going on. These days, I tend to speak up. I try to do it kindly, but ultimately, I don't see how it is useful for people to spend their time at work this way."

~~~~~~

Five suggestions for practicing asteya

1. Create a time log for a day or a week, and note each time you are late to a meeting, spend time talking about things that distract from your work, send a lengthy email when a short answer would do, etc. How much time was lost to such activities?

2. List things that might be viewed as "taking what is not freely given." Next to each item on your list, jot a few notes about what is lost when you or others unconsciously "steal" something that is on the list.

3. Choose a habit to give up or create that would help you live out the precept of asteya. Focus on it for three weeks. Journal about what changes.

4. Make a list of what you would gain and what you might lose if you committed to practicing asteya.

5. Share your intentions to practice asteya with a few trusted coworkers, and ask them to give you feedback when they see you doing things that are not aligned with those intentions.

NON-SQUANDERING OF VITAL ENERGIES
(*Brahmacharya*)

Continence, restraint

The two paths lie in front of the man.
Pondering on them, the wise chooses the path
of joy; the fool takes the path of pleasure.

From the Katha Upanishad

Dina was browsing in the boutique of a trendy, popular yoga studio in Scottsdale, Arizona. She'd arrived early for the Saturday morning class because it often got crowded and she wanted to snag her favorite spot near the door. But the previous class was still in *savasana*, and the studio doors were closed. As she perused the merchandise on the sale rack, she overheard the conversation of two men in their early twenties. One had expressed surprise to see the other.

"After I left you last night, I figured you'd be too wasted to show up for an early yoga class," said the first young man. His friend laughed, admitted he was fried, then began to chronicle the exploits of a Friday-night bar hop.

As the studio doors opened at last, Dina caught the tail end of the men's conversation as she gathered up her things to go in. "That sounds like a wild and crazy night, man," said the first young man. "You must be exhausted."

"I am definitely tired, but I didn't want to miss this class," was his friend's reply. "I'm going out again tonight, and I need to detox to retox."

Brahmacharya is probably the most notorious of the *yamas*. It's frequently framed as a command for celibacy, particularly for men (which affects women, of course!). In ancient times, the "voluntary loss of semen" was seen as squandering precious vital energy that was better expended on devotion to God, self-realization, and absorption. Swami Sivananda emphasized this aspect: "*Brahmacharya* is absolute freedom from sexual thoughts and desires. It is the vow of celibacy. It is control of all the senses in thought, word, and deed."

It is hard to imagine that the ideal reflected in the first part of his statement is always desirable or could be easily achieved—in ancient times or modern. Most modern yoga scholars acknowledge that interpretations of *brahmacharya* that center on celibacy or on sexual activity for procreation only are too narrow and impractical. Most yoga practitioners are householders who have no intention of taking monastic vows.

Indeed, the yoga world has not been immune from sex scandals, including some that involved high-profile gurus known for their preaching about sexual chastity. Talking about this precept, a yogini we interviewed for the book said, "I find it distracting and disingenuous to take sex advice from people who have been involved in sex scandals."

Her point is well taken, and sex scandals have become such a part of the cultural fabric that many people have developed a callous attitude about them. No one, including us, wants to condone bad behavior, but in our view it's also important to separate teachings from the fallible human beings who teach. While many have succumbed to temptation, the Sutra itself is clear that sexual energy should be mindfully harnessed.

Mahatma Gandhi, who experimented with celibacy in his later life, talked about *brahmacharya* as "control of the senses in thought, word, and deed. There is no limit to the possibilities of renunciations. . . . For many, it must remain as only an ideal."

Nischala Joy Devi, a doctor, yogini, and author who studied with yogi sage Swami Satchidananda for twenty-five years, translates *brahmacharya* as "living a balanced and moderate life." We also like the practicality in the definition used by Jaganath Carrera in his book *Inside the Yoga Sutras: A Comprehensive Source*. He explains the precept as "the avoidance of non-productive expenditures of energy."

SEX AND THE WORKPLACE

Swami Satchidananda advised that by practicing sexual continence, "we preserve not just physical energy alone, but mental, moral, intellectual, and ultimately, spiritual energy as well." It's easy to lose sight of that in modern culture.

Films and television, books and magazines bombard us with stories of sexual intrigue in the workplace. The popular series *Mad Men*, for example, is an example of *brahmacharya* violation run amok: chain-smoking, cocktails at 10 A.M., trysts in hotel rooms during the lunch hour, and males and females leering at each other in ways that tell you work is not the central thing on their minds. That sort of human drama provides limitless possibilities for popular entertainment. But such shows also demonstrate how "absent" these people are from their work—literally and figuratively. (Also in the absentee column are *ahimsa*, *satya*, and other yogic precepts.) The consequences of the characters' actions engender a great deal of human misery that is representative of what exists in the real work world. Stories abound of the ways office affairs and romantic entanglements have wreaked havoc with people's lives and the work environment. We have experienced it ourselves. In my younger days, for instance, I was far too cavalier about the power of sexual attraction and rarely gave sufficient consideration and respect to the myriad consequences that could unfold from making unwise choices in this arena.

This precept doesn't require that you abandon a healthy sex life or the hope of finding your soulmate at work. Because people spend a majority of their time on the job, it's often the most likely place to meet people. This brings up three serious considerations for the practice of *brahmacharya*—flirting and dating, honoring committed relationships in the workplace, and developing healthy relationships with coworkers. Sexual attraction is a powerful urge and a powerful force, and sex is an act of intimacy and potential creation. The karmic consequences are almost impossible to predict in the early throes of attraction. When you bring this aspect of being human into the workplace, it is advisable to be thoroughly mindful about it.

Elizabeth held several corporate jobs before becoming a full-time yoga instructor in 2006. She is happily married now, but recalls the thrill of the romantic conquests she once had at her office job. Flirting, dating, becoming entangled with someone new was fun, and made her more interested in work—sort of. In the beginning of the relationships, when things were new and exciting, "The anticipation of seeing that special someone meant I couldn't wait to get to work. And I think I saw myself as wanting to be a better employee, but mostly so the boss would praise me, which would make me look even better to my suitor."

Unfortunately, when the relationships went awry, she had the opposite reaction, and work was the last place she wanted to show up. "I wouldn't even want to take a shower, much less go to work. And when I got there, instead of being productive, I would sit around thinking about that person all day. I'd be sad, disgruntled, and hard to get along with."

Relationships can cause difficulties "even when they last forever," notes Elizabeth, and we can speak to that personally. It takes constant vigilance for Jamie and me not to let our personal issues spill over into our business partnership, and we're not always successful. Obviously, we can't in good faith say that people in an intimate relationship should never work together. But we do see the wisdom of *brahmacharya* and being extra mindful about the consequences of unleashing your sexual energy at work.

CONTROL AND CONSEQUENCES

Maureen Dolan, a professor at DePaul University and an ordained priest in the Kriya Yoga tradition, says the essence of *brahmacharya* is a practice of sexual responsibility. Living this practice means taking control of your sexual and emotional urges and considering the consequences before you act on them.

"For those who have taken a vow of celibacy, it means refraining from sexual activity. For those who have a partner, it means fidelity. For those who are single and engaged in sexual activity, it means practicing safe sex by taking precautions to avoid disease and unwanted pregnancy," says Dolan, who writes for *YogaChicago* using her ordination name, Swami Shraddhananda.

Taking action against rape, sexual harassment, molestation, or other sexual violence or irresponsibility also is *brahmacharya*. If you see someone being sexually harassed in the workplace, *brahmacharya* would ask you to act. Dolan adds, "You wouldn't just walk away from someone being sexually abused. You would be compelled to do something about it."

Embracing and integrating the other *yamas—ahimsa* (non-violence), *satya* (truth-telling) and *asteya* (non-stealing)—will help you live out *brahmacharya* and naturally guides your approach to relationships at work. Embracing these precepts culminates in healthy, respectful relationships that center on your well-being, as well as that of co-workers and the work environment.

CONTROLLING CRAVINGS

Brahmacharya also speaks to controlling sensual cravings—those deep longings or yearnings we have to satisfy one or more of our senses. When you consistently cave in to your cravings, it fosters creation of unhealthy habits that facilitate non-productive expenditures of energy. Yearnings are not necessarily a bad thing. A useful question when it comes to these desires and habits is "Who is in control, and how does this craving serve me?" If you are expending energy on things that don't really contribute to developing your potential, that waste time, harm your health, or interfere with good relationships, that runs counter to the practice of *brahmacharya*.

Charles Duhigg, a reporter at the *New York Times*, wrote about enslavement to a mid-afternoon chocolate chip cookie habit in his book, *The Power of Habit: Why We Do What We Do in Life and Business*. Over time, his cookie cravings caused him to gain eight pounds and eventually got the attention of his wife, who began making pointed comments.

As Duhigg set out to understand the intractability of habits, he did a series of experiments that revealed a surprising conclusion. He discovered his craving was attached to a reward, but it wasn't the cookie. It was the socializing he did when he ate the cookie. Once he discovered what the true reward was, he was able to replace the mid-afternoon sugar fix with a quick stretch at his desk and a chat with a nearby coworker. After a few minutes, refreshed by the break, he returned to work. His cookie cravings went away, he gained time, lost weight, and we presume, his wife's pointed remarks were directed elsewhere.

Duhigg's findings illustrate the power of habits, or *samskaras*, described by Dr. Timothy McCall, the medical editor of *Yoga Journal*, as "thoughts, words, and deeds that are repeated over and over" even when they don't serve us. These *samskaras* actually etch themselves into your brain. Research has shown that changing or breaking habits changes brain patterns, creating new neural pathways. Some cravings are esoteric and more difficult to see—a hunger for power, for example. A voracious appetite for attention or affection, or pining for praise from your boss and coworkers all have ramifications for how you approach your work.

An existence free of cravings releases "a vital energy of consciousness," according to Swami Jnaneshvara Bharati, an American-born yogi who was ordained a monk by Swami Rama in 1993. Your strength, capacity, and vitality all benefit from a strong practice, he says.

Jacob, an executive leadership coach and yoga practitioner, uses this concept with clients, although he doesn't tell them it is *brahmacharya*: "I emphasize how important it is not to waste their physical and mental energy on thoughts, actions, and activities that are either out of their control or not in service of their intentions. These are all distractions from the 'being' they are trying to cultivate."

~~~~~

Five suggesions for practing brahmacharya

1. Spend a week noticing interactions between the genders at your workplace. Do you see flirting? Assertion of power based on gender? Stereotyping? Make a list of what you notice. How do these interactions serve or interfere with effectiveness and productivity?

2. Make a list of the sensual cravings that are non-productive or interfere with health or well-being. Observe for a few days when they assert themselves, and note the time and place. Can you identify the reward that comes from satisfying the craving? Jot down some notes on why that reward is so compelling.

3. Make a list of some of the consequences of satisfying your cravings. Looking over the long term, what benefits have resulted? Have any of them borne consequences you're not happy about?

4. Spend a day or two keeping track of thoughts, impressions, and comments you make about the opposite sex. How many could be considered sexually provocative? Jot a few notes about your experience. What do you notice?

5. What do you stand to gain by managing your sexual energy and controlling your senses at work? What do you stand to lose?

NON-GREED
(*Aparigraha*)
Generosity, living simply

~~~~~~~~~~~~~~~~~~~~~~~~~~~~~~~~~~~~

Affluence is not a matter of what you have but what you don't lack. If your needs are satisfied, that is the ultimate state of affluence.

Pico Iyer

~~~~~~~~~~~~~~~~~~~~~~~~~~~~~~~~~~~~

While traveling in Chicago several years ago, I attended a yoga class in a small studio. As the room became crowded, people looked around uncertainly, trying to find space to put down their mats. In the front corner of the room, one early arrival had created a commodious compound on the wood floor, surrounding her mat with a barricade of props. Sitting serenely on her mat in lotus pose, head bent and eyes shut, she seemed oblivious to the whispering and shuffling of mats, blankets, and bolsters as people tried to create a place for others to practice in a room filled almost to capacity.

Finally a brave soul knelt beside the woman, interrupting her reverie with a slight touch to the shoulder. "Please excuse me," she whispered. "Would you mind moving your mat over a little so I have a place to put mine? We've run out of space."

The woman's head jerked up, her eyebrows slammed together, and she retorted through tight lips, "No, I won't! I get here early on purpose so I have plenty of room for my practice. Maybe *you* should try it."

In the tense silence that followed, the would-be practitioner, her face hot and unhappy, hastily gathered her things and fled from the class.

❀

When Jamie and I got married, we asked a friend to sing Don Henley's "For My Wedding" just before we took our vows. It's an unconventional choice—the song talks about setting aside romantic sentimentality and recognizing the difficult and serious endeavor of marriage. I particularly love the beginning of the chorus, which speaks to the practice of *aparigraha*: "To want what I have, to take what I'm given, with grace." *Aparigraha* is about that. It asks you not to covet, or hoard, or possess more than you truly need.

When your gaze becomes fixed on gratitude for what you have, it is easier to curb your appetite to acquire. Cultivating a willingness to share resources, viewing them as abundant rather than scarce, creates a healthy detachment that ultimately benefits the whole community as well as you. No matter how vast the world's resources may be, if we are taking more than we need, we are depriving or exploiting someone else.

The modern work landscape is littered with object lessons of human greed as a key motivator. Wealth is often seen as *the* sign of success, a shiny golden bauble that, if captured, guarantees comfort and happiness. Once riches are acquired, it becomes easier to rationalize that those who lack the necessities are in that state solely because of their bad choices or because they lack a work ethic.

The wanton pursuit of wealth is one of the key sources of global misery, and in reality, not a sustainable business practice. Natural resources are controlled by the rich and powerful, while those who work to mine, harvest, and collect often barely get by. Economies are based on an engine fueled by ever-increasing consumption. Advertising bombards us with messages of more, *more*, MORE and we listen, with no regard as to whether we already have enough. Taking what we want, instead of what we need, has ravaged the planet that our lives depend on, putting all living beings in jeopardy.

WORK MOTIVATED BY LOVE AND SERVICE

At many workplaces, practicing *aparigraha* would call for a fairly radical collective mind shift. The world of work most people grew up in reveres the shiny golden bauble and sees grasping at it, achieving it, as proof of hard work. In the United States, consumer spending is considered a "production" statistic. Acquisition is applauded. People explain this tendency toward greed as merely "human nature." When people made this argument to yoga sage Eknath Easwaran, he would gently disagree:

> *You are debasing human nature. I am elevating it. The best work is done not though the profit motive but through love. . . . We have such affluence and abundance in this beautiful land that I cannot understand why there is poverty, why children should be without food and shelter, why millions of men and women, skilled and ready to work, are unable to get jobs. Even an untrained economist like me cannot fail to see that this is not an economic order, but an economic disorder.*

There is a divine aspect to work in both process and outcome. The *dharma*, or purpose, of business is to "create wealth for the society and serve the customer," says M. S.

Srinivasan, a yoga scholar, but only as long as the work engaged is virtuous.

CONFUSING PLEASURE AND PROFITS WITH PURPOSE

In the Sutras, Patanjali talks about *asmita*, a type of ignorance that confuses the physical body and conscious mind with the higher, divine self, or spirit. One of the ways this manifests, says Marzenna Jakubczak in a 2004 article published in the *Journal of Human Values*, is through the mind saying, "This is *mine*. *This* is mine. This *should* be mine." It becomes a mantra.

When you're motivated by the need for pleasure or ego satisfaction, you find a way to justify the sacrifice of almost anything, including your integrity, your dignity, or the respect of loved ones. People who are ruled by greed won't be able to help themselves. They covet, deceive, and hoard "in the hope that pleasure may be repeated, prolonged, or perpetuated forever," Jakubczak says. But that pleasure does not necessarily result in happiness.

Research has provided scientific evidence that, once basic needs are met, there is little correlation between the amount of money possessed and reported happiness. Indeed, people are more likely to find happiness and satisfaction by sharing what they have rather than hoarding it. In a study done by Elizabeth Dunn of the University of British Columbia and Michael Norton of the Harvard Business School, researchers asked students to hand out $20 bills to people. Half of the recipients were instructed to buy something for themselves, the other half to spend it on someone else or give it away. In the follow-up, "those whom we told to spend on others report greater happiness than those told to spend on themselves," Dunn and Norton wrote in a *New York Times* article. "And in countries from Canada to India to South Africa, we find that people are happier when they spend money on others rather than on themselves."

The false belief that causes people to chase wealth robs them of other valuable things, such as time and energy that could be invested in things that truly bring happiness. Like family. Like hobbies and the pursuit of knowledge or skills. Or volunteer work for a church or worthy cause.

Practicing *aparigraha* does not ask that you set aside your natural desire for fulfillment and well-being, aspiration and ambition. It does, however, make a distinction between working for what you need to survive and thrive, and the temporary pleasure of acquisition for its own sake. Eknath Easwaran again: "I am not suggesting there is anything wrong in a businessperson making enough profit to support his or her family in comfort—everyone should have this opportunity. But we have exaggerated the importance of profit out of all proportion to its natural place in business. We have become addicted to it, and that is a very dangerous situation."

In his *Conquest of the Mind* he adds, "I am not pleading for poverty but praising simplicity."

IMPLICATIONS AT WORK

The ways people have been asked to work, and the systems and procedures that have been designed to keep work moving, typically don't foster a perspective of abundance.

Think about the ways people view and manage their budgets at work. As the end of a fiscal year approaches, what happens if there is money left unspent? You must find ways spend it! It seems foolish to do otherwise when the system tells you that if you don't spend it now, you will be deprived later. And what if you were to suggest giving your department's surplus to another department that is facing a shortfall? Well, that's just crazy talk.

Money is where the mind goes first, but the practice of *aparigraha* at work is about more than getting your hands on lavish amounts of lucre. Consider how easy it is to get attached to things that don't even really belong to you: *my* office, *my* desk, *my* supplies, *my* project, *my* budget. We recently worked in an organization where several people were deeply unhappy in the wake of reorganization that meant some managers would lose their offices and have to work in cubicles. I was sympathetic—I remember similar feelings of loss and umbrage in a similar situation at a newspaper where I worked. But if you can learn to be resolute to the impermanence of *everything*, and understand that material stuff doesn't really matter, you'll avert self-inflicted suffering.

At her restaurant job, Rebecca says people often view the work itself from a scarcity perspective, even in times of abundance. The trendy restaurant where she works is always crowded. People show up to dine early to make sure they get in, and on the weekends, people line up in the street, waiting anxiously for a table. With all these big-spending customers, servers make good money, yet the grumbling grows when the owners announce they will be hiring new people to ensure top-notch service.

People get squirrelly, Rebecca says. They think about what they might lose without considering that those hired also need to make a living. And it doesn't stop there. "I've seen people who are just obsessed about who has what shift, and which section. Honestly, they're not even thinking about the numbers realistically. [The restaurant owners] hire more people to handle the business because it is growing. That allows us serve more people efficiently, which helps ensure the success of the restaurant. In the long run, it doesn't really end up affecting anyone in a financially negative way. But people choose to go around unhappy when they could choose to be grateful for the good living they are making."

LEARNING TO LET GO OF YEARNING

Rebecca says if she is not attentive to her practice, the "attitude of gratitude" she tries to cultivate can quickly devolve into attachment to wanting more than she needs. Yoga helps her keep things in perspective—the way she chooses to view tips is an example. The staff pools all tips, and at the end of a shift, the manager divvies proceeds among those who worked. The system is designed to foster teamwork and better customer service. Even so, people get consumed with the number next to "gratuity" every time they look at a paid bill.

"Most of the servers go around celebrating or complaining about every single tip they get. For a long time, I was making myself crazy by doing it, too. If I didn't get the tip I thought I deserved, I'd start fuming about it." Then she started paying attention to what was actually happening.

"You know what? It always evens out at the end of the night," Rebecca says. "We always go away with 18 to 20 percent in tips. So why do I want to make myself unhappy if one tip isn't as much as I think it should be? Now I try not to look at what my customers left. In the end, it doesn't matter, because I want to give everyone my best service based on who I want to be, not what tip they might give."

Do you yearn for the status that a corner office gives you? Are you unhappy unless you have the latest, greatest technology? Maybe your job depends on the latest version of the current Big Thing, but can you make the distinction between that and lobbying for an upgrade just to satisfy your desire to be cutting edge? Do you deprive your family of time and attention in order to have a bigger house, better vacations, the latest clothes and gadgets? Attachment to anything—perks, a parking spot, a promotion, *more stuff*—rolls you away from *aparigraha*.

Observing *aparigraha* becomes easier when we can learn to stay in the moment, with a clear vision of where we are and what we need right now. Letting go of attachments—to our desires, to material objects, to the need for attention—is easier when you "want what you have, and take what you're given with grace," as the lyrics to Don Henley's song point out. It fuels a more equitable distribution of resources, and douses the flames of envy and dissatisfaction.

Rebecca says *aparigraha* practice has helped shift her perspective about why she works. "I'm there to create a good experience for my customers. My yoga practice has helped me see that everything always works out. The more we trust, the less we need to worry. I am earning a good living. I can pay my bills and support my son. I can manage. It's enough."

Five suggestions for practicing aparigraha

1. Make a list of the reasons you work. Put them in order of importance. What do you notice?

2. Reflect on what would change if you operated from a view of abundance rather than scarcity. What are the internal and external pressures that keep you from "wanting what you have"?

3. Keep a gratitude journal. On a regular basis, take a few minutes at work to jot down at least one thing for which you can be thankful.

4. When the desire for something you do not have arises, examine your motivations about acquiring it: "Is this truly a need or just a want? Why do I want it? How will my life be better by acquiring this? Could I be content with what I have now?"

5. Commit to a daily generous act at work, giving something and expecting nothing in return.

three

THE SECOND LIMB: PERSONAL CODE OF CONDUCT

~~~~~~~~~~~~~~~~~~~~~~~~~~~~~~~~~~

Personal transformation can and does have global effects.
As we go, so goes the world, for the world is us.
The revolution that will save the world is ultimately
a personal one.

Mary Catherine Bateson

~~~~~~~~~~~~~~~~~~~~~~~~~~~~~~~~~~

THE *NIYAMAS*

By now, you have a sense of how interrelated the *yamas* truly are. Violating one *yama* inevitably involves negative action in another. Practicing one strengthens and supports the practice of the others. *Ahimsa* (non-violence) cannot be achieved without *aparigraha* (non-hoarding) and practicing *aparigraha* makes it impossible to violate *asteya* (non-stealing). Practicing *satya* (truth-telling) will help you honor *asteya* (non-stealing) and *brahmacharya* (managing vital energies).

Michelle Ryan, who owns a yoga studio in Florence, Massachusetts, says practicing the *yamas* informs every aspect of her business. "I try hard to incorporate *ahimsa* in what I do, compassion for students and where they might be in their lives. I also try hard to be truthful (*satya*). I am honest with students about what they can and can't do physically, and also about what I do or do not know! I am conscious about not sharing others' ideas as if they are my own, which is *asteya*. And I do not look at my students as dollar-signs walking through the door, *aparigraha*. From a business standpoint, that may not make much sense to some people. But I am not teaching for the money—although it's nice when that manifests, too!"

This same symbiotic relationship exists within the *niyamas*, which outline a personal code of conduct. They are beneficial individually, and like pieces of a puzzle, they combine to create something wholesome that will help you be ethical, productive, and serene at work.

The five precepts are:

Saucha—cleanliness, purity

Santosha—contentment

Svadhyaya—self-study

Tapas—discipline, energy, zeal

Ishvara-pranidhana—surrender

Practicing these five powerful precepts will have subtle and profound effects on the way you see others, and the ways you approach work. The individual observances minimize the external distractions that become obstacles to developing your full potential, and block you from recognizing the potential in others. The *niyamas* will help you be present to your own life.

As Cat de Rham and Michèle Gill wrote in their beautiful book, *The Spirit of Yoga*, "When we work selflessly, the mind stays pure. While we are not indifferent to the result of our actions, we are not addicted to its fruits. Actionless action is a slow but important process of learning to rely on the strength and equanimity that comes from within. From the Self."

PURITY
(*Saucha*)

Cleanliness, unsullied

The only cure for materialism is the cleansing of the six senses (eyes, ears, nose, tongue, body, and mind). If the senses are clogged, one's perception is stifled. . . . This creates disorder in the world, and that is the greatest evil of all.

Morihei Ueshiba, founder of Aikido

Before Mary began teaching yoga full-time, she worked in a four-star restaurant in Phoenix that caters to the rich and the powerful. She was one of only two female servers in an environment awash in testosterone, starting from the chef on down to the dishwashers. Their female presence was tolerated, but they didn't always feel welcomed or valued. Mary felt like she had to act tough to survive in this high-stress, male-dominated environment.

One day, as she was entering a studio for a yoga class, she was surprised to see her female coworker emerging from the previous class. "Wow! I didn't know you did yoga!" Mary said. "When did you start practicing?"

Her coworker smiled. "Actually, I started doing yoga because of you." Mary's surprise deepened. She had never suggested her coworker try yoga.

"It's true," her coworker said. "I figured it was doing *something* for you, because you stopped swearing in the kitchen."

Saucha is the precept of purity. At its most basic level, it speaks to hygiene: your body, your mind, and your environment. Keeping your body clean may seem like a no-brainer, until you stop to appreciate how this simple act affects so many things. The act of cleaning can be soothing and creates a sense of accomplishment. Bathing can calm and refresh you. Cleanliness protects you from disease and discomfort. Washing your hands might seem like a trivial example, but it prevents the spread of germs. Healthier people mean fewer sick days.

A friend once told me how she watched in amazement as one of her coworkers carefully wiped down the puddles on the bathroom sink counter at work, water that had been splashed by others who had washed their hands before her. "Why are you doing that?" my friend asked. "You didn't make that mess, and anyway, we have a janitorial service."

"I know," her friend replied. "But it only takes a minute, and makes it nicer for the people who come in after me. It makes me feel better to wash my hands at a clean sink, and I imagine other people feel the same way."

CLEANLINESS, HEALTH, AND WELL-BEING

Yoga speaks about purity on many levels. One of the purposes of an *asana* practice is to purify yourself internally. *Pranayama* (breath control) can aid in cleaning the lungs, and the physical practice builds *tapas* (heat), said to help cleanse the organs and muscles. Yoga asks you to be mindful about the kinds of foods you choose for nourishment—will they pollute your body or cleanse and strengthen it? Many yogis adopt a vegetarian or vegan diet as a way to practice both *saucha* and *ahimsa* (non-violence). These things could have a positive aspect on your work.

Stephanie, who has practiced yoga for many years, says committing to *saucha* connects her to well-being, energy, and health. "There was a time when I was overweight and sluggish, and pretty much caved in whenever I got cravings for food that I knew was bad for me. But yoga helped me realize, finally, that this is the only body I am going to get in this life. It sounds trite, but I did start seeing my body as my temple. When you look at it that way, it seems ridiculous not to take good care of it, to purify it, in a sense. That led to a change in how I ate, how I exercised, and how I felt. People at work have noticed that I have way more energy and focus."

If you have an on-the-mat yoga practice, you may have noticed how it changes the way you see your physical being. For me, it's been a wonderful discovery of my body's ability to support me—it is capable of far more than I would have imagined. Like Stephanie, I've begun to realize the positive choices I make about the food I eat, and the exercise I get is a way of honoring my body for all it does for me. While I don't consider myself a fanatic, I am far more attentive to what I put in my mouth—choosing water or tea over Dr Pepper, for instance. Jamie and I try to eat fresh, organic fruits and vegetables, in balanced portions. When we don't, I can tell the difference. I am more easily fatigued, bleary, easily distracted. It's much harder to concentrate on my work, and I am far less productive. We also do a master cleanse twice a year to rid our bodies of toxins, twelve days of forgoing all fermented foods, dairy, refined sugar and flour, and eating lots of fresh organic produce, whole grains, and fish. Jamie describes the resulting feeling: "Lighter, refreshed, and so energized."

EMPTY THE GARBAGE IN YOUR BODY AND MIND

Yoga can help you create a mind body awareness that helps you see and feel the consequences of eating food that isn't good for you, or noticing your frame of mind after you let loose a string of angry curses. In that way, yoga becomes a better motivator than doctor's orders or the advice dispensed in books or magazines, because it emanates from your own internal wisdom.

A clean mind is another aspect of *saucha* that will allow you to work more effectively and serenely. Judie, a journalist who has practiced yoga for more than a dozen years, says she thinks about "emptying the garbage in my head before I go into work." She makes an effort to let go of petty resentments and clears her head of negative self-talk.

Choosing her vocabulary carefully is another way Judie incorporates *saucha*. "I have become really careful about saying things like, 'I hate going to those meetings' or 'I could have killed her for missing deadline.' I guess that also is a way of paying attention to *ahimsa* (non-violence) but I also think it keeps my mind more pure because I'm not thinking about or using violent or hateful metaphors. I'm not perfect at it, but I think that being mindful about it makes me feel more peaceful and compassionate toward my coworkers."

Like Mary, Judie has broken the habit of swearing when she is frustrated or angry—not an easy thing to do in a newsroom environment where profanity is often employed as verb, adjective, and punctuation. She takes a deep breath or two instead of responding in the heat of the moment, which helps break the *samskara* (habit) of swearing when things don't go the way she wants them to. Judie says she started swearing to fit in—everyone did it, so it must be cool. But her yoga practice led her to think about what she was getting out of it and how it could make others around her feel. Sure, they were only words, but after committing herself to *ahimsa* and *saucha*, cursing felt like a violation.

At a mindfulness meditation retreat I attended in 2011, one of the teachers told the story of her friend who earned a living as a long-distance truck driver. He had chronic back pain, and the doctor recommended yoga as a form of physical therapy, for healing and to prevent further injury. He started doing it for his body, but soon found himself going deeper with more practice and study. After awhile, it began to influence his behavior on the road.

Being behind the wheel for days and nights at a time, the truck driver was witness to many a crazy maneuver and actions that ranged from rude to risky. Road rage was as common as the billboards that line the highways. Before yoga, his favorite response to drivers who aggravated him was to lay on the horn, swear angrily, and/or make an obscene gesture. After yoga, he began to notice that those reactions never made him feel better, they just amped up the emotion. He decided to break that habit and replace it with a more hygienic response. Now when he gets cut off in traffic, he takes a deep breath, smiles at the driver, and says out loud: "May you know happiness and deep well-being." The teacher added that not only has her friend's back healed, he no longer dreads being on the road. He enjoys looking for opportunities to wish others happiness, even if they are unaware of an anonymous truck driver's blessing.

PURITY AT YOUR DESK

At work, the precept of *saucha* can be extended to your environment. A cluttered, disorganized workspace can be a recipe for distraction and inefficiency. A neat, clean, and well-organized workspace has aesthetic and practical appeal, and you can be more productive if you know where to find things when you need them. This was my mother's theory, and I resisted it for years (sorry, Mom!). However, once I started to develop the habit of putting things back in the same place, cleaning up immediately after doing a project, and creating a filing system that allowed me to find information quickly, I had to admit Mom was right. Your mind is more likely to feel more spacious if your desk isn't buried in detritus. Being organized is a habit that can help you save time and circumvent frustration. If you know where to find what you need, when you need it, you'll save time and energy and keep frustration at bay.

You might even find yourself swearing less.

Five suggestions for practicing **saucha**

1. Do an inventory of your eating habits, keeping a journal if it is useful. Notice what makes you feel healthy and energized, and what makes you feel heavy or sluggish.

2. Consider honoring "your temple" by giving up for one week a food or drink that pollutes your body, such as soda or sugary foods. Notice how you feel. Slowly increase the number of days per week where you are committed to eating fresh, nutrient-rich food all day.

3. Make a list of the harsh, violent, or profane language you use, when you use it, and how others respond

when you do. Notice how you feel. What do you stand to gain from eliminating this kind of language from your conversations? What do you stand to lose?

4. Decluttering and organizing your environment at work doesn't have to become an all-day project. Choose one shelf, one drawer, one corner at a time. As you go through your belongings, useful questions to ask include, "When did I last use this? What is my plan for this? Might it be more useful to someone else? Is this something I need or just want?" This can help you make decisions about what you really need to keep.

5. Think about work situations that create negative energy. What is your contribution? What things hook you in a way that make you cave in to the negativity? Make a list of practices that could help you dispel negative energy more quickly.

CONTENTMENT
(Santosha)

Fostering gratitude, non-attachment

~~~~~~

There is no end of craving. Hence contentment
alone is the best way to happiness.
Therefore, acquire contentment.

Swami Sivananda

~~~~~~

As people in the class settled their torsos over their thighs in *paschimottanasana* (seated forward bend), Michael shifted and squirmed, trying to perfect his pose. He wanted to lengthen his upper body a bit more, so he bent his knees to create space in his lower back. Then it bothered him that his legs were not straight, so he backed out of the pose a bit.

Glancing around at his neighbors in the class, he saw he was the only one who couldn't reach his feet, so he pulled his belly a little tighter and began crawling his fingers toward his ankles. He circled his head, trying to release the tension in his neck.

From the front of the room, the teacher spoke softly but firmly: "Try to stop doing, and just be."

He did not know if she was looking at him, but Michael felt she was speaking to him, and he got the message. Shushing the perfectionist chattering in his mind, he smiled as he relaxed into a perfectly acceptable *paschimottanasana* pose.

Contentment (*santosha*) is the *niyama* that asks you to be content with who you are, where you are, and with whatever you have. It is our true human condition, according to many sages and gurus, but gets buried under layers of ignorance, ego, and attachment.

Santosha has a close relationship with non-greed (*aparigraha*) and is key to the integration of all the benefits yoga offers us. Contentment is always within us to find, once we learn how to stop, breathe, and tap into it. In a world where titles, social status, money, and the material trappings of success are so emphasized, work environments offer lots of opportunities to develop your capacity for *santosha*. But that doesn't make it easy.

When you focus on contentment, it's much easier to devote your full attention to the tasks at hand, keeping in mind the purpose for which you show up to work each day: to develop your own potential and that of others. That gets derailed when you begin wishing for things to be other than they are. Why can't the boss be more competent? Why are customers so difficult? Why are my colleagues so annoying? Try turning such questions on their head. What can I learn from the mistakes I see others make? How can I serve this difficult customer with compassion and kindness? How can I practice tolerance or be curious when others do or see things differently than I do?

"A cheerful mind is transparent. It allows you to see what is right and what is not right. . . . It will allow you to see that life is simple and very meaningful in and of itself," says Pandit Rajmani Tigunait, spiritual director of the Himalayan Institute, an international non-profit organization dedicated to fostering yoga, holistic health, and other spiritual practices. A strong practice of *santosha* becomes a guiding signal, helping you know when you are taking right action, he says.

CHOOSING CONTENTMENT

In many of the organizations where Jamie and I have worked, people give us a big pushback on the notion of having the ability to choose your response to the circumstances in which you find yourself. While you might have an immediate or instinctual emotional response to disappointment or frustration, the decision about what to do with those feelings is all yours. Choosing optimism, accountability, and commitment in the face of fear and inevitable disappointment is not only possible, it is necessary for success. It breeds *santosha*.

"But we don't have a choice!" people argue. This tells us that they do not feel in control of their work lives, and that is understandable. Jobs are constantly changing because of fluctuations in the marketplace, technology, reorganizations, and customer demands. As you watch colleagues get moved, demoted, or laid off, it's only natural to become fearful that it could happen to you and feel helpless to do anything about it.

Many of my former newspaper colleagues have been caught up in that kind of marketplace change. One of them, Rae, told me that her yoga practice helped keep her sane as she watched the numbers in the newsroom dwindle in a series of layoffs. The people who survived each round were demoralized and wondered when their day would come. Some people coped through the use of prescription drugs for depression and anxiety. Rae says staying connected to breath helped her cope with the uneasiness. "It was a pretty stressful time. Everyone around me was afraid, and it created this negative pool of energy, which I could see was attracting similar energy in me. I figured it was just a matter of months before I was laid off myself. I think I got deeper in my practice because of what was going on, and it rewired me to think differently. I realized I had a choice about whether to eat from the negativity that other people were dishing out around me."

She also worked to let go of judgment, because she understood people's moods and actions were rooted in fear. "Working on being more compassionate helped me focus on the good in people," Rae says. "And it kept me from freaking out when I watched things get blown out of proportion."

Feelings of fear, disappointment, and helplessness at work are completely legitimate. No one has control over a fickle marketplace. No one can ensure your long-term prospects. You may not always fully grasp the reasoning behind the decisions top leaders are making.

Yet even in the face of all these things, you absolutely *do* have a choice about how you bring yourself to work. One of my yoga teachers, Mary Beth Markus, exemplifies *santosha*, and a recent story from her life is an example about the power of choice in the face of difficult circumstances. Mary Beth and her husband, Vince, have owned and operated Desert Song Yoga and Massage Center in Phoenix for thirty years. They've always rented studio space, but dreamed of owning something permanent. In the wake of the real estate collapse of 2008, the couple decided to buy and renovate a building even though it would be a strain on their financial resources. As I was doing the final revisions for this book, I received an email with distressing news. While doing renovations at the new studio, Vince had fallen from a 12-foot ladder, breaking his wrist, dislocating his shoulder, and shattering his cheekbone. He required surgery and would be out of commission while he healed, which meant time and money in a situation where they could ill afford it. That happened on a Saturday. The following Monday, Mary Beth's mother, brother, and extended family, who live on the East Coast, hunkered down under the onslaught of Hurricane Sandy. Her brother lost his home, and many of her close relatives also suffered serious losses and damage to their possessions.

I frequently attend her Wednesday class, and in the wake of all that bad news, I did not expect to see her teaching that week. But when I walked into the studio, there she was, smiling, serene, and ready to teach. As she related the dramatic events to those in class, her composure and calm were unwavering, and she never once complained. Mary Beth spoke of gratitude—that Vince hadn't been more seriously injured. She told us how he kept apologizing profusely as she rushed him to the hospital, and all she could tell him, again and again, was how much she loved him. She was thankful that her family members in New Jersey had all survived, alive and safe—stuff could be replaced. While the setback to the construction schedule on the new studio was a disappointment, Mary Beth smiled and said, "It will get done eventually." She even rejoiced at the prospect of having found a few yoga recruits. "The people in trauma [at the hospital] were all asking me, 'How are you staying so calm?' I told them, 'Yoga. It's all about the yoga.'"

THE ATTITUDE OF GRATITUDE

Santosha is a close companion of *aparigraha*. Actively taking an inventory of what you have, and feeling grateful for it, helps you stay connected to non-greed, which is one of the most effective ways to foster contentment. While many people think that *more* will make them content—more money, a nicer house, more frequent vacations—research shows that only a small percentage of our overall happiness can be ascribed to our circumstances. How we choose to view any given situation is far more likely to influence our level of *santosha* than the circumstances themselves. Viktor Frankl's famous work around life and meaning, beautifully chronicled in *Man's Search for Meaning*, illustrates this lesson, and had a profound influence on Jamie and his late partner Joel Henning as they began developing materials for their consulting business.

One freedom that can never be taken from people, Frankl realized in the misery of Nazi Germany's concentration camps, is their choice about how to face the circumstances in which they find themselves. Frankl's message of the power of choice also is exemplified by people such as Mahatma Gandhi of India, Martin Luther King Jr. of the United States, Nelson Mandela of South Africa, and Aung San Suu Kyi of Myanmar. They refused to let the most unjust and brutal circumstances douse their fires of contentment, and their optimism and serenity were catalysts for movements that altered history.

Attachment is something that can derail *santosha* lickety-split, and is one of the chief causes of disappointment, hurt, and anger. Swami Satchidananda, in his translation of Patanjali's Sutras, observes that the mind "has a duty to desire"—life can't be experienced without yearnings and attachment. What will trip you is to attach ego to your desires. "Pure, selfless desire has no expectation whatsoever, so it knows no disappointment no matter what the result."

If you can channel desire into doing good work for its own sake, without attachment "for the resulting fruit of actions," you're far more likely to uncover *santosha*. The *Bhagavad Gita* says, "Do not consider yourself the creator of the fruits of your activities; neither allow yourself attachment to inactivity. Remaining immersed in union, perform all actions forsaking attachment to their fruits, being indifferent to success and failure. This mental evenness is termed 'Yoga.'"

That is difficult advice to follow in the demanding modern workplace, to be sure. We are constantly told to be attached to the fruits of our labor, especially in a work world where the vernacular is peppered with phrases like "management by objective" and "measurable outcomes." Neither is it realistic or necessary to think that you should not set goals or strive to achieve them—dedication to excellence is an admirable quality. It's counterproductive to think that contentment translates to inactivity or passivity. The secret is to strive for excellence while recognizing that even if plans get upended and projects fall apart (as they surely will), you still can choose to practice *santosha*. As Rod Stryker writes in *The Four Desires*, "Attachment to desire, not desire itself, is the underlying cause of practically all of our pain and suffering. . . . [it] is the source of pain we experience when we fail to fulfill a particular desire. It also is the source of the anxiety we feel when we do fulfill a desire but fear we may lose what we have achieved."

It is a logical way to live, if you think about it. In reality, even with the best intentions and hard work, we can never be in control of how things turn out. Consider two teams who are playing each other in a match. Both teams may be at their peak excellence and functioning at the highest level, yet they can't truly control the outcome of the match. Too many other factors will influence the final result. That doesn't mean they set aside their aspirations or stop giving their utmost effort. Nor does it mean they can't choose to be content if the other team wins.

Banishing attachment takes great courage and persistence. You are, however, in control of your actions. Eventually my friend Rae was laid off, just as she expected. "I went through a major freak-out because it was the first time in my adult life I didn't have job security or health insurance. Experiencing those emotions—disappointment, anger, fear—was only natural. I know that, and I don't think yoga is about not having those feelings. Even so, my yoga practice helped me more quickly let go of the destructive aspects of those emotions. Anger and resentment and wishing things were otherwise were not going to bring me peace. Because of yoga, I think I have been able to more quickly focus on the ways losing my job might also be providing me opportunities." In addition to becoming a yoga teacher, Rae has channeled her artistic creativity into starting her own business.

DETACH FROM YOUR STORIES

Santosha is often derailed by the stories you tell yourself. Seeing your stories as "truth" will lead to all kinds of difficulty. In our consulting work, for example, we advise people to be curious about and investigate what their coworkers' facial expressions or actions mean, instead of getting agitated by what they think is going on. When emails go unanswered, instead of getting angry that your coworker is being rude, check it out. Maybe they've been out sick, are overwhelmed by the workload, or the emails were inadvertently sent to a spam folder. Don't ruin your day by attaching yourself to a story about someone else's motives and intentions. When you choose connection, and investigate what is going on, you might be surprised by what their stories reveal.

Jamie remembers getting frustrated with a new consulting client, an executive who, as he saw it, was "blowing off" training sessions that were required of the team that reported to this leader. After Jamie had juggled multiple schedules and finally settled on dates for two workshops for the team, he was chagrined and a little angry to discover their leader wasn't going to be there due to "schedule conflicts." The executive did, however, make himself available for a pre-workshop interview, and that is when Jamie discovered that the poor man was working two high-level jobs simultaneously. This executive was transitioning into his new role leading a reorganized division of a global company, while also keeping up with his old job as vice president of sales for one of the company's subsidiaries until his replacement was hired. Once Jamie knew the executive's story, the irritation vanished, replaced by feelings of compassion.

Lacey says that one of the biggest mental challenges in her law enforcement career has been learning to suspend judgment about the behavior of the people she deals with. It isn't useful to see them as bad or evil, no matter how counterproductive or dangerous their actions are. People usually act in ways that make sense to them, she says, even if she doesn't understand their motivation. Admittedly, it's not easy to have compassion for the person who is firing a deadly weapon at you, but Lacey works hard to remind herself, "I don't know their story. That gives me perspective and helps me not to take things personally. It helps me feel more peaceful, which makes me be more effective."

Thomas, who supports people with disabilities, says remembering that all people are divine helps shift his mindset when his judgments get in the way of *santosha*. "Just because you don't see the divine in people doesn't mean it isn't there. I have developed the habit of looking closer at people, looking deep into their eyes for that spark. When we help the world function better, we feel better about ourselves. And that generates contentment."

Five suggestions for practicing santosha

1. Notice the times you start feeling agitated at work. Jot them down, including the time, place, and circumstances. Who was present when the agitation began? What were the circumstances? What do you notice after you've reflected on these events?

2. Think about a time you were angry with a colleague or disappointed by a decision that was made at work. What story did you tell yourself? What other stories might have been possible? What could you do to consider a different story as a way of practicing *santosha*? What is a story you are telling right now about a work experience?

3. In moments when you're unable to find *santosha*, read through your gratitude journal if you have one or add to it. What changes?

4. Think about a time you were disappointed by results at work. What would you gain by letting go of your attachment to specific outcomes? What do you have to lose? What is compelling about thinking you can control how things turn out?

5. For a few days, notice what stories you tell yourself when things don't go the way you want them to. Reframe those stories without changing the outcome. What do you notice?

DISCIPLINE
(*Tapas*)

Energy, zeal

~~~~~~

We are what we repeatedly do.
Excellence, then, is not an act, but a habit.

Aristotle

~~~~~~

I had shoulder surgery in 2008, and ever since, I wait for that moment in yoga class where we are directed to take our mats to the wall for an inversion pose. That is a cue to hold my breath and chant a silent mantra: "Please don't let it be handstand. Please don't let it be handstand."

After physical rehabilitation and many months of exercise and yoga, my shoulder is strong again—in some ways stronger than before. I've regained the ability to do postures I once feared were lost to me. I pop up into a headstand (*salamba sirusana*) with relative ease, and I consistently rock a passable *chattaranga* (a form of push-up). With patience and perseverance, the forearm balance *pincha myurasana* is something I no longer dread.

But I have yet to get back my handstand (*adho mukha vrksanana*) without a significant assist from my teacher or a fellow yogi. I am frequently tempted to head for the ladies' room when the time comes, or just give up trying altogether. And yet I do not want to be ruled by fear. Even if I never do another handstand in my life, persevering in the attempt is good practice.

So when the yogis around me drag their mats to the wall for handstand, I silence the negative mantra, and remind myself: *It is not just about the destination. The journey is equally important, and practice is action.*

I attempt a handstand.

꽃

The translation of the Sanskrit word *tapas* is heat. Swami Kripalu, an India-born guru who advanced the teachings of Kundalini Yoga in the Western world, likens this precept to the friction caused by "going against the grain," which initially causes pain or discomfort. Developing self-discipline—practicing *tapas*—is about leaning into the distress that often accompanies an attempt to learn something new or the churning experienced when trying to change cherished but unproductive habits. *Tapas* helps you "burn off" the things that don't serve you.

As with the other *niyamas*, *tapas* calls for presence. On the mat, this quality helps you hold a challenging pose, even as your muscles quiver and your mind begs for relief. Without the vital tools of self-awareness, self-discipline, and concentration, your potential remains untapped or underutilized. Pema Chodron, an American Buddhist nun and author of *When Things Fall Apart: Heart Advice for Difficult Times*, says *tapas* brings you back from "any form of potential escape from reality." When you are reluctant to experience the pain of doing something you are unaccustomed to, *tapas* asks you to embrace the discomfort to foster growth. T. K. V. Desikachar says that *tapas* is what helps you move forward.

Christopher began practicing yoga soon after enrolling in college. It fostered a *tapas* that helped him cultivate the mental focus he lacked in his first few semesters. Once lackadaisical about schoolwork, he created study habits that improved his grades and a mental discipline that continues to be useful in his job. After taking up yoga, he made the dean's list. "Yoga helped me commit to my studies. It really helped me sort everything out—not just my muscles and how I was feeling physically, but also my energy."

Maureen Dolan, who teaches a class on yoga at DePaul University, defines *tapas* as the "enthusiastic discipline" that fuels follow-through and excellence. "It is the forgoing of immediate personal gratification for something larger and more worthwhile, and of benefit to more people." Eknath Easwaran says that *tapas* is what makes "spontaneous excellence" possible and is an essential practice for training the mind for vigorous mental disciplines such as meditation. Anyone can learn, he says, if they are prepared to put in the effort.

CHANNELING THE FORCE

Zoe, who teaches first-graders at a public school, says she uses yoga techniques to help instill that "enthusiastic discipline" into her young students. They have a natural zeal for learning, but are short on self-discipline. She uses breathing techniques (*pranayama*, the topic of Chapter Five) to help her students harness and perpetuate their natural *tapas*.

"Kids are full of energy, so you want to keep that fire, enhance that fire, but not let it burn out of control," says Zoe, who also teaches yoga to adults in the evenings. Myriad rules and regulations require her to adhere to a specific curriculum in the classroom. Because what she teaches is so prescribed—and how she is judged depends so heavily on how much students learn—helping the first-graders stay on task is essential.

"Kids in a small classroom feed off of each other, especially after lunch or recess when their energy is very high. You have to find a way to contain that and even bring it down, so they can find the discipline to focus on their work," Zoe says. She doesn't call it yoga—she calls it "deskercize."

The children like it so much they promise to be on their best behavior if Zoe will please, please, please let them do it. Using breathing techniques, meditation, or physical poses, she can generate energy when it is waning or lower the levels when the kids are wired.

"For instance, I might dim the lights, and have them close their eyes, and put their hands on their bellies. Then I tell them to see if they can blow up their bellies like a balloon, and see if they can deflate the balloon very slowly by breathing out through their noses. Slow inhale, slow exhale. After a minute or two, the whole energy has changed. They are ready to settle down and get to work." They've tapped into *tapas*.

REGENERATION TO RESTORE THE FIRE

The paradox of *tapas* is that generating the heat and energy also requires conservation and renewal. Rest is essential. Those 12-hour days you're putting in might seem essential for meeting deadlines and getting the work done, but how does it ultimately serve you or the workplace if you become exhausted? When you show up feeling physically stressed, mentally tired, or emotionally resentful about sacrificing important parts of your life, you suffer, and so does your work.

Time is a finite resource. Until someone discovers a way to manufacture more of it, the humble and the mighty all get twenty-four hours per day. Time management might help you pack more activity into your day (if packing more activity into your day really enriches your life), but it won't give you twenty-five hours.

Going slow in order to go fast will serve you far better than getting stuck in energy-sapping overdrive. Taking time out for reflection and introspection helps keep the flame of *tapas* going. I love the story told in a yoga class that makes this point:

> *A student went to a sage with this question: "Master, if I stay with you and study to deeply understand your tradition, how long will it take?" The sage thought for a moment and replied, "Ten years." Dismayed, the student said, "But what if I work very hard, and study day and night without ceasing? Then how long will it take?" Again the sage reflected before he answered, "Twenty years."*

Happily, you have at your disposal a resource to help you be more effective and feel better, and it's completely renewable—energy. As Kevin Cashman writes in *Leadership from the Inside Out: Becoming a Leader for Life*, "Although each day brings almost impossible demands on our time, with too many meetings, obligations, and 24/7 connectivity in a global marketplace, it is our energy and resiliency that are stressed daily, not the clock."

What sounds more realistic, squeezing more time out of the day or investing in strategies that will increase your energy? What do you notice about your choices, your environment, and your productivity levels when you are feeling strong and energetic? What can you do to manage your energy in a way that allows you to maximize your contribution at work? If you are feeling beat up and drained at the end of your work day, what needs to change to get your fire burning again?

No matter how much you love your work, too much of it can throw your energy, and your life, out of whack. Lots of simple strategies can help restore it. A walk around the block. Five minutes of meditating. A yoga class after work. Listening to music. Or, like Zoe's first-graders, maybe you just need to reconnect to your breath. Restoring your energy will help banish resentment, clear your mind, and make you more effective at work. (We offer some breathing techniques at the end of Chapter Five.)

Tapas is an internal fire and can only be lit from within. In a world of work riddled with motivational literature and seminars promising to teach you how to "motivate others," it's easy to get sucked into the notion that someone else should incentivize you to action.

Understanding *tapas* means accepting that you are in charge of your own motivation and morale. *Tapas*—like motivation—only works when it is intrinsic. By its very nature, it must be self-generated. The support and encouragement you receive from others is a wonderful gift, but ultimately you make the choices about the quest for learning, the quality of your work, and whether to push the limit of perseverance or pause for energy renewal.

You tend the fire.

~~~~~

Five suggestions for practicing tapas

1. Developing self-discipline requires self-awareness. Commit to a day of jotting down the times you think you should be doing something (studying, working out, reading) but don't. How many of these things are tied to your goals or values? How do you end up deciding what to do?

2. If you're having a hard time feeling enthusiastic about your job, make a list of things that would help you feel more motivated and instill discipline. What do you notice? How many of the things on your list are dependent on the actions of others? How many are within your control?

3. Make a list of your typical daily activities, and then draw two columns next to the list. On one column, write "Energy Draining" and on the other "Energy Restoring." Go down the list and put check marks in one of the columns next to each activity. What do you notice?

4. Next time you hear yourself saying: "I can't do this because . . ." change the wording to "I choose not to do this because . . ." What do you notice?

5. Choose a long-term desire you want to satisfy or must stretch to obtain (i.e., paying off a credit card, getting a promotion, or extending an aspect of your yoga practice). Make a list of what you might have to give up to achieve the desire. Make a list of what you would gain.

SELF-STUDY
(*Svadhyaya*)

Reflection, introspection, self-awareness

〰〰〰〰〰〰〰〰〰〰〰〰〰

To find out who you truly are, you have to inquire.

Jiddu Krishnamurti

〰〰〰〰〰〰〰〰〰〰〰〰〰

Los Angeles offers a smorgasbord of yoga practices, teachers, studios, and styles. Susana, who works as a film director, likes to partake of the buffet. In a given week, she can do hot yoga in downtown L.A., Shabbat yoga on the beach, drum circle yoga in the hills, or a gentle class in her neighborhood. When she rolled up her mat at the end of each class, she would find herself thinking, "This is *exactly* the class I needed."

While reflecting one day on her eclectic practice and the positive influence yoga has had on her life, Susana had a surprising insight about her practice. "It's not that there is some sort of 'yoga angel' directing me to the right classes based on what I need. What I now realize is my inner spirit knows that wherever I am practicing, that is where I am meant to be. Even when I feel annoyed by the practice, or I don't like the sound of the teacher's voice, or someone next to me makes strange noises every time he's in downward dog, I remember: "Be humble. I am in yoga class! I am grateful. I am alive."

🪷

Consciously cultivating increased self-awareness is a practice of *svadhyaya*, the fourth *niyama*. It asks us to incorporate self-study as a regular practice, with an intention of assessing ourselves both lovingly *and* critically. This will help you develop the clarity needed to make mindful, positive changes in your life.

How is self-awareness cultivated? Reflection, introspection, and consistent study are the building blocks of *svadhyaya*. Barclay Hudson, my professor and mentor, says the best way to start this practice is by stopping: Stop *doing* and invest some time in *being*.

You can't practice *svadhyaya* without making a conscious choice to step off of life's treadmill—at least for a little while—to catch your breath, gaze into your internal mirror, and do personal inventories. Too often, work demands keep people excessively engaged in external activities. And don't count on your boss or coworkers to urge you to slow down or take an hour or two away from the office for self-reflection. You're tied to a perpetual to-do list that never seems to get shorter. How is it possible to take stock of who you are and create intentions about who you want to become when you're constantly running, trying to catch up to your life?

Yet self-study is imperative if you mean to spark your light to ever-increasing brightness. You can't fully develop your potential without awareness—of faulty assumptions, your contribution to a difficult issue, or habits that do not serve you. Such awareness, combined with yearning for a more desirable state, is the provenance of positive change.

Svadhyaya contributes to creativity, self-awareness, emotional intelligence—essential qualities for a satisfying and successful work experience. William George, former Medtronics CEO and co-author of *True North*, says it is a practice that helps people get connected with their authentic selves. In an article published by the Harvard Business School, George writes: "Authenticity is developed by . . . understanding one's life story and the impact of one's crucibles, and reflecting on how these contribute to motivations and behaviors. As people come to accept the less-favored parts of themselves that they do not like or have rejected, as well as learning from failures and negative experiences, they gain compassion for themselves and authenticity in relating to the world around them."

INTERNAL FOCUS, OUTWARD GAZE

Laura Karet became the CEO of her family's multi-billion grocery business in 2011, succeeding her father, David Shapira. "He was incredibly successful. It is a daunting thing when you're following big shoes." In addition, her father remains chairman of the Giant Eagle board, so he's not just her dad—he's her boss. "It's truly a wonderful thing," she says, "but it can also be frustrating."

A longtime yoga practice has inspired her vision for the company, Karet says, and its practices help her stay grounded. She often uses connection to breath to inspire "mini-sessions" of *svadhyaya* when she finds herself responding instinctually to situations instead of taking mindful action. Karet recalls an incident where such a session helped her glean an important insight about not letting her emotions rule. She was on her way to give a speech to a group of business people when her assistant called to announce that her boss/dad had scheduled a board meeting at the same time she was slated to deliver her presentation. "I was mad! He knew I couldn't be there, and I started fuming. If I had been a CEO hired from the outside, he never would have done that. How could I be a CEO who isn't at a board meeting?" She called her dad, who apologized, but she continued to fume. Then she reminded herself to take a deep breath and think clearly. Was this who she wanted to be? "I realized he didn't intend this to be an affront to me, and the topic of the meeting wasn't even something I really needed to be there for." While she was happy to have the insight, Karet said she's committed to continuing *svadhyaya* to develop a self-awareness so keen that she can check her emotions *before* they cloud her perspective. "Having the ability to be conscious of where you are, what you are good at, and what you're not so good at—and being okay with it—is a big part of being a good leader."

The Yoga Sutras say that "study, when it is developed to the highest degree, brings one close to higher forces that promote understanding of the most complex." Finding sources of inspiration, whether it is studying the effectiveness of leaders or coworkers, reading inspirational texts, or seeking knowledge that helps us stretch our abilities, are also practices of *svadhyaya*.

Susana says she receives abundant edification from her yoga teachers that inform her work. "In a place like Los Angeles, yoga is a great way to keep your ego in check. They *never* hand out trophies at the end of class," Susana says. "The other thing is that even though my favorite teachers are very different, the one thing they have in common is that they are the truest versions of themselves.

"As an artist and human being, I find this really inspiring in my own work. When I am directing, there is a natural inclination to want to do *everything* myself. Really, my job is to help the crew to realize maximum creative potential. My favorite yoga teachers have helped me realize that in order to be a real influencer, you must allow yourself to be influenced. This muscle of adaptation has really been developed through my yoga practice."

Sometimes a simple observation, if you are mindful, can become an opportunity for profound reflection. As I was writing this chapter, a friend emailed me a copy of a blog post by Peter Bregman, author of *18 Minutes*. The blog post was about an experience of witnessing a father speaking sharply and unkindly to his son, after which the boy turned to his sister and hit her. That inspired Bregman to wonder about misdirected anger, and he began to think about the times he had done that himself.

"After seeing that boy hit his sister, I began to watch myself more closely. What do I direct at one person that's meant for another?" Bregman wrote. "It's hard to see that kind of behavior in yourself. At first, I didn't notice anything. But I kept looking. . . . A pattern began to emerge, one I'm embarrassed about, but that became hard to ignore: I do and say things specifically to impress people, even people I don't know."

Bregman went even deeper as he gazed into his internal mirror. Did he *really* care what complete strangers thought of him? And whom was he really trying to impress? His reflection revealed a childish wish to please his mother. With this insight, he was able to begin changing his habitual reactions. *Svadhyaya* helped him notice and understand a nonproductive behavior, which helped him choose to make a positive change.

THE SEEDS OF CERTAINTY

Self-awareness helps you to deconstruct the myths that have been sold to you as truth. What are you certain about? And why? Have you held up to the light your beliefs and philosophies, or stood them on end to consider a different perspective? People tend to cling to certainty because they think the opposite is uncertainty. In reality, the opposite of certainty is curiosity, openness, and willingness to see something in a fresh way. *Svadhyaya* asks you to find a child's mind, and examine what you have seen a thousand times before as if it were a brand-new discovery. Does that mean you have to give up skepticism or thinking about things critically? Absolutely not. Study requires the duality of openness *and* skepticism, as the great scientist Carl Sagan pointed out in an essay published in 1987: "It seems to me what is called for is an exquisite balance between two conflicting needs: the most skeptical scrutiny of all hypotheses served up to us and at the same time a great openness to new ideas. Obviously those two modes of thought are in some tension. But if you are able to exercise only one of these modes, whichever one it is, you're in deep trouble."

Leigh Ann, who has practiced yoga for twelve years, credits *svadhyaya* with helping her process work feedback in a way that leads to a higher quality of contribution in the office. She doesn't always see things the way her managers and coworkers do, but she makes a point to examine their feedback, and her reaction to the feedback, before she responds.

She contrasts that habit to the instinctual response she had after her first personnel review at a company specializing in relocation services. "I got an 'average' rating, and I took it very personally. I was angry and hurt. My attitude towards the company totally changed, and I didn't last long after that. Looking back, a lot of that feedback could have been useful if I had just stopped to think about it for awhile." Yoga has helped her be less self-centered, Leigh Ann says, and now she considers feedback in terms of how it can help her, and the company, perform better. "I'm not sure if my impulse to question authority will ever disappear, but I process constructive criticism much differently now. I've developed an attitude of curiosity and gratitude, which has brought me more respect at work. My coworkers call me the Zen master."

Reflection, introspection, and clarifying your intentions about who you want to be and what you want to create at work are all about *svadhyaya*. This practice helps you bring your authentic self to work. Too often, clarity around intention gets overlooked in the rush to answer the question "How?"

How do I work more efficiently? How do I make the team perform better? How do I motivate others? How can I get the promotion? How can I make more money? Such questions are not unimportant, but they can be answered in a more meaningful context if you've first wrestled with questions about who you want to be in the world. What do you want to contribute? What would you like your legacy to be? As clear answers emerge, it is easier to choose the attitudes and actions that support your intentions. Self-awareness will help you understand how your beliefs and behaviors connect to the enterprise you are serving.

Svadhyaya can also help you develop confidence in the strengths that you already possess. Not just your knowledge, skills, and techniques (although they are certainly important) but also the essence of *who you are*. Larry Dressler, author of *Standing in the Fire*, asserts that knowing and understanding your "way of being" can make the difference between competence and mastery: "It is a specific kind of presence that others experience as fully engaged, open, authentic, relaxed, and grounded in purpose." *Svadhyaya* helps you find that core of integrity and presence so you can call it forth in complex, heated, and demanding situations.

Dawna, a physician who started out working in emergency rooms, says this precept of yoga helped her face a crisis early in her career. She considered herself a rookie at the time, but "at least I had enough experience that my nightmares about making a bad decision and killing someone had gone away."

The ER where she was working required that patients wait no more than thirty minutes after arrival to be seen by a caregiver. Depending on the number of patients demanding attention, the seriousness of their maladies, and the number of caregivers working, that could be tricky.

One day, things were so crazed that Dawna ended up with three patients in a row, all complicated, high-stress cases. The first patient was on dialysis and had below-the-knee amputations due to complications from severe diabetes. She had a fever and was vomiting. She spoke only Spanish, which required Dawna to get a translator on the phone. As the patient began to explain her symptoms to the translator, she threw up all over the phone.

Excusing herself and promising to return, Dawna went to the next examining room, where a five-year-old boy had a fever of 105 degrees and, between sobs, kept screaming that his stomach hurt. He also was vomiting, and his mother spoke only Spanish. Another translator would be needed.

Dawna walked out of the examining room, knowing the clock was ticking and she had yet to see the third patient. "I started freaking out. I kept thinking, 'I can't do this—it is too overwhelming. I am in over my head!'" She managed to get through the shift, but soon after was notified by a medical committee that some of her patients had filed complaints. She would have to appear before the committee to address the issue.

"I had already done a lot of thinking about that day," says Dawna, who has practiced yoga for more than a decade. "Although I always considered myself really approachable, for the first time I could see that when I get overwhelmed, I start snapping at people. I'm not always so nice at a time when people need a calm and compassionate response. And I also realized when I got that stressed out, I didn't take very good care of myself, which just made everything worse."

She went to her meeting with the committee, feeling embarrassed and humble instead of defensive. She acknowledged that the patients who complained had cause, and she apologized for the way she had treated them. "I was honest about that, and I also apologized for wasting their time. I told them that I hadn't been taking care of myself, but that I was committed to doing things differently. I promised to make sure that I eat during my shift, and also drink plenty of water." But she didn't stop there. Dawna mustered up the courage to tell the committee that in order to do her job effectively, she would not be able to consistently comply with the demand to see patients within thirty minutes. Sometimes that just didn't serve the patients, she told the committee.

Svadhyaya practice helped Dawna see how she was contributing to a difficult situation and own it publicly. At the same time, she wanted the medical committee to understand that the hospital's rules were unrealistic, which gave her the courage to practice *satya* by speaking truth to power. "I wanted them to understand the real-life impact of their demands on us. I told them, 'I intend to address this on my own, and as an organization, I think you should consider addressing this as well.'"

Dawna's story has a happy ending. The response from the committee was favorable, and she has never received another patient complaint. "Honestly, I didn't need anyone to tell me what I had done wrong or how to fix it. Through my practice of *svadhyaya*, I figured it out myself. And by having the courage to be direct with the members of that committee, I was showing them a human face that revealed the real impact of their demands. It made a difference."

~~~~~

Five suggestions for practicing svadhyaya

1. Use this *niyama* to reflect on this book so far, and see what you are learning about yourself.

2. Write down three things you believe are true at work. Identify the assumptions in your statements. Spend a few minutes asking yourself, "What if it weren't true? Is there a different story I could tell?" How many other stories are possible?

3. Make a list of all the labels you associate with yourself or which other people have used about you (husband, mother, worker, American, immigrant, hard worker, difficult to get along with, etc.). What are some of the inherent assumptions of those labels? How do they influence the way you engage work and the people you work with? Are there labels you wish to add or to shed? Which ones and why?

4. Ask a few close and trusted friends or coworkers to give you feedback when they see you resorting to bad habits or taking actions that don't reflect who you want to be. Set aside a specific time for periodic conversations to get feedback. When you receive it, don't justify your actions, just say "Thank you." What do you notice?

5. Make a list of your core values. Where did they come from? Are they still relevant? Now think about examples where these influenced your actions. Have there been times when you failed to align your actions with your values? Why?

SURRENDER
(*Ishvara-pranidhana*)
Connecting to something larger than Self

~~~~~~

Don't push the river. It flows by itself.

Robin Caasdan

~~~~~~

When her yoga teachers invite her to set an intention for practice, Jessica's routine is to silently recite a standard list:

1. Clear and peaceful mind

2. Authentic loving speech

3. Open compassionate heart

4. Powerful inspired intuition

5. I am that I am

During a period of transition that had left her feeling confused and off balance, she decided one day to let go of her customary mantra and invite something beyond herself to reveal a new intention. The word that emerged in her mind was *expansion*.

"It was so clear," Jessica says. "I had this profound realization that I need to expand." Surrendering to her subconscious, she noticed the intention created a subtle shift in her attitude and movements throughout the *asana* practice. "We did Warrior II, and I felt the energy expanding from finger to finger rather than just a sensation of lifting my arms. Every pose I did felt physically expansive. This intention also inspired me to think about the metaphor of expansion and what it meant to my life, what it was I wanted to do next. It was wonderful. Once I surrendered my need to recite the same intention, something spoke to me, and I got an important insight into something about my life that needed attention."

✿

Ishvara-pranidhana is often translated as "offering the fruits of one's actions to the divine." This *niyama* is about surrendering to the life force or the supreme, which we interpret to mean our higher selves—the perfect, constant light that resides within you. It shines always, waiting to be uncovered as you open yourself to the possibilities of endless expansion.

Surrender is not an easy precept to embrace, especially in Western culture. The word can send shivers of apprehension up the spine. From the time we are born, we are immersed in a world of competition and superlatives: Be the smartest, the fastest, the brightest, the prettiest, the most accomplished. Know all the answers. Messages about the importance of winning are constantly flooding your senses, in both concrete and subtle ways. When you don't get your way, when your desire is thwarted, when you're passed over for a raise or a promotion, it feels like a loss, drenched in discouragement or humiliation. No wonder people back away from the concept of surrender—it has become synonymous with defeat, failure, and loss of control.

Ishvara-pranidhana practice means devoting yourself to doing your very best—without being attached to outcomes—and recognizing that you are part of something larger than yourself and embracing that expanded reality. "When people surrender, they stop sweating the small stuff and see the big picture," says Maureen Dolan. "A sense of freedom expands in body, mind, and spirit. The sense of our interconnectedness becomes more profoundly realized."

LETTING GO OF ATTACHMENT TO OUTCOMES

Detachment from outcome is about channeling your highest intentions, consistently choosing to align your actions with those intentions, and then surrendering to the knowledge that events, circumstances, and outcomes will always be out of your control. Getting attached to a certain result only causes agitation and suffering. Even if you get what you want, worry sets in that you might lose it.

Letting go is a concept Jessica has learned to find useful in her work as a coach and educator. She describes her work as helping adults, mostly working professionals, "transform themselves to higher levels of maturity and self-awareness." Consequently, she also constantly seeks ways to raise her own level of awareness.

As part of her "expansion," she recently took a class that centers on ways to create self-awareness, evoke collective insights, and spur positive action in large groups. In the final session of class, the teachers asked students to engage in "conversational painting" by doodling during a conversation to see what emerged.

Jessica chose to use watercolor pencil because it is harder to control, and she wanted a media that would foster an organic and intuitive experience—a kind of surrender. "As I doodled, I decided to trust. I didn't decide or think about what would come out of it. I let go to see what would emerge." She scribbled as she listened to people, then smeared the scribbles with a few drops of water. As the water and pencil markings blended, she thought, "Oh my goodness, this is someone in a Warrior II pose!"

She began wondering why that image was emerging, so she did a search for "yoga warrior" on her laptop. The answer she got: *A spiritual warrior who bravely does battle with the universal enemy of self-ignorance and ego, the ultimate source of all our suffering.* The metaphor was powerful.

"That's one of the things I try to help people do when I work with them. From working on myself, I've learned that I need to let go. I need to learn to surrender to the larger purpose of the group I'm working with," Jessica says. "At the same time, I realize that doesn't mean I can slack off or have a lack of accountability. I'm still required to do intense preparation so I can bring the best of myself."

But after preparation is done and she goes to work, "I know I have to walk into the space and release the need to control. Processes have a life of their own. My work is to stay present with them, to use my professional skills to shape [the process] while realizing something bigger is going on. And I have let go of an attachment to the outcome."

The practice of *ishvara-pranidhana* helps dissolve ego. Surrender sets the stage for uniting with your higher self in a way that generates inner peace, compassion for others, clarity, and freedom. Getting yourself disentangled from the emotional hook of "wanting what you want" will help you be ready to learn the lessons imbedded in whatever life hands you. And when life hands you a setback or a disappointment, in that moment, you have the opportunity to choose how to face those circumstances, instead of falling into counterproductive cycles of blame, cynicism, and helplessness. In the *Bhagavad Gita*, Krishna advises Arjuna to remain dispassionate: "The ones I love . . . stand above the sway of elation, competition, and fear. They are detached, pure, efficient, impartial, never anxious, selfless in all their undertakings." Krishna also extols the virtue and benefit of surrender: "Better is surrender of attachment to results, because there follows immediate peace."

SURRENDERING TO RESISTANCE

An important aspect of yoga concerns overcoming resistance. *Ishvara-pranidhana* is one expression of that. Work gives you abundant opportunities to practice, because success depends on everyone surrendering their selfish desires to a vision of doing what is best for the whole. Surrendering to "that which is greater" means aligning your actions with what is best for the enterprise, instead of making decisions focused only on what is good for your career, your team, your department. Practicing *ishvara-pranidhana* helps you take responsibility for understanding the big picture. It becomes an imperative to connect your work contribution to the mission of the business.

One way to "surrender" your desires to the good of the whole is to become deeply informed about your workplace. What is the marketplace you serve, and who are its customers? What is the vision of the enterprise where you work? What are the interdependencies with other departments? What kind of relationship with your customers and stakeholders needs to be created to be successful?

Shifting your perspective from what you want to what the whole needs is a different way of looking at accountability. Instead of only asking, "Did I complete the tasks of my job assignment?" the question expands to "Did I do my best to serve the whole business?" Instead of asking, "How do we hold *them* accountable?" recognize the power in asking "How am I choosing to be accountable to the whole?" If you're acting on purely selfish desires, it becomes a violation of *aparigraha* (non-greed).

As you become devoted to this practice, the persistent voice of "What about me?" recedes. You discover ways to unite your actions with the higher purpose of service as a means of fulfillment.

Two yoga teachers that I study with regularly, who have decades of experience between them, often share stories about their experiences with resistance. They talk about the times they developed an urgent need to go to the bathroom, or take a water break, when it was time to do a posture they didn't like. For them, the reward for surrendering to resistance is learning to love the offerings of the pose. Such stories make me smile, because I have often resisted in similar ways in yoga class and in life. Instead of opening myself up to a new experience that looks hard or scary, when things get tough I sometimes look for ways to disappear. I don't say, "I'm too frightened to attempt this," or "I am worried about failing and looking foolish." Instead, I do something else—procrastinate, make excuses, organize a closet—and rob myself of discovery.

My yoga teachers say frequently that achieving a perfect posture or learning to enjoy a pose is not the point. This aspect of yoga is about acknowledging fear, discomfort, or reluctance and overcoming ego as you surrender to something new and expansive. Even if my teachers had never achieved the poses they disliked, they knew they would learn something about themselves if they stayed present during the attempt.

It is no different at work. How often does your fear of change lead you down the path of resistance, sometimes without even realizing it? What do you do when you really don't want to surrender to another, to the wishes of the project team, or to a demand from the marketplace? Instead of relinquishing your fears or selfish desires, how do you behave? Maybe you don't show up for meetings. Maybe you "forget" to answer emails. Maybe you question others' credentials or knowledge about the task at hand. Maybe you change the subject, or go for the cheap laugh. Everyone has his or her favorites.

What would change at work if you acknowledged your fear or hesitation directly, then committed to surrendering to something new? At work, you may discover that surrender is not a dirty word—it requires courage and great strength.

In yoga class, you might end up in a handstand.

~~~~~

Five suggestions for practicing ishvara-pranidhana

1. Make a list of the meanings and associated feelings evoked by the word "surrender." Do you see it as positive, negative, or dependent on the situation? How does your view affect the actions you take?

2. List the gains you would get by practicing *ishvara-pranidhana*. What are the associated losses?

3. Remember a time when you refused to surrender at work. How did it turn out? If you see the results as a loss, think about what might have changed if you had surrendered. If you perceive a gain, can you see a

hidden loss? Bring to mind a time you surrendered—willingly or unwillingly. What differences do you observe in each of these cases?

4. What things, people, roles, or outcomes are you attached to? Make a list and think about the reasons you are attached. Is a person or job role central to your sense of worth? How would cultivating a healthy detachment change the way you see yourself? How would it influence your work?

5. Invest time in noticing how you feel when you begin to attach yourself to an outcome—anxious, irritable, fearful, agitated? When those emotions begin to surface, what can you do to stay in the present? Consider developing a mantra that can help you keep non-productive fretting at bay, such as "I am doing the best I can. The outcome will be what it will be. I can let go."

four

THE THIRD LIMB:
POSTURES
(*ASANA*)

~~~~~~~~~~~~~~~~~~~~~~~~~~~~~~~~~~

You must learn to be still in the midst of activity
and to be vibrantly alive in repose.

Indira Gandhi

~~~~~~~~~~~~~~~~~~~~~~~~~~~~~~~~~~

In the last stage of my journalism career, I was lucky enough to work for a newspaper that provided space in the office building for a weekly, hour-long yoga class and paid for a teacher. At 6 P.M. on Tuesday evenings, a dozen or so of us met in a designated conference room, then moved the furniture to create space for our mats.

The class was always in danger of being canceled if our numbers dropped too low. When I would troll my coworkers to look for recruits, I always emphasized the physical and mental benefits of practicing yoga postures. Knowing they were a cynical bunch, I would add, "Mark [Roberts, our teacher] sometimes talks a little woo-woo, but you don't really have to pay attention to that part. Just let it wash over you."

In actuality, I had no idea how thoroughly I was being soaked. I loved listening to Mark, most especially when he prepared us for *savasana*. He used exotic terms that I didn't fully understand, such as *pranayama* and *pratyahara* and *samadhi*. The strange words fascinated me.

Because working for a daily newspaper calls for crazy hours, it wasn't uncommon for me to return to my office after yoga, where the newsroom was busily engaged in creating the next day's report. I usually felt reenergized, yet calm and ready to focus—and it was the best time to recruit. People who popped into my office to discuss a story or ask a question would sometimes say, "Wow. You are glowing." I would reply with a smile, "Yoga. I am full of the life force!"

Mark's classes were so meaningful and intriguing that I began regularly attending the other classes he taught around town. The spiritual approach he incorporated into the *asana* class lit a spark in me. I noticed a shift in my mental state, which affected the way I viewed my colleagues and my approach to work. The spark burned steadily brighter as I continued to practice with Mark and other teachers. I'm convinced yoga helped give me the confidence and courage to apply for a fellowship to teach in South America and then leave a career—as satisfying as it had been—to explore other possibilities that might better feed my soul.

Eventually, this burning yearning led me to the first yoga teacher training I did in 2005–2006. The physical practice became a gateway for exploring all the limbs of yoga, which, as I mentioned in the introduction, aligned perfectly with the philosophies underlying the work of the new career I was launching at the same time.

Historically, the Third Limb of yoga was not considered the most significant, although in the Western world it certainly has become the most practiced and familiar. *Asana* was intended to prepare the body for the long periods of focus and meditation necessary to achieve absorption—union with the ultimate reality, enlightenment. In the West, an on-the-mat practice is the typical introduction to yoga, another tool in the arsenal of fitness routines to help the body increase flexibility and balance. Some are attracted to the physical practice as a method of stress reduction. The beauty of an *asana* practice, however, is that it provides a window onto the rich landscape all eight limbs have to offer, should you choose to open your eyes.

Deanna, a development editor who lives in the Midwest, experienced this transformation as her physical practice took root and blossomed over more than twenty years. She says the yoga principle of alignment has helped her both on the mat and off. "Alignment is probably the thing I think about most in my practice, because it has so many layers and meanings. When I am on the mat, alignment helps me get the most from my body, ensures that I don't injure myself, and keeps me healthy and grounded," Deanna says. "It's equally important for me to be aligned with my work spiritually and emotionally. When I take on a project, I have to know it is aligned with my values, both in terms of the content and the person I am working with."

There have been times in her career when she wavered, taking on work she didn't think was a great fit, because "everyone has to put food on the table." But after yielding to that temptation a few times, the experiences led her back to her core values—alignment always come first.

Lawrence, a soldier serving in Afghanistan, says he appreciates the way his *asana* practice has kept him in good physical condition for his demanding work. "I am one of these people who was graced with a short, stocky stature, and I really abused my body physically as I was working and growing up. The stretching techniques I learned in yoga helped me regain a lot of flexibility and have increased my core strength. That helps a lot when you're in the military."

CORPORATE BENEFITS

An on-the-mat practice serves people in myriad ways, and companies are beginning to recognize this. Several well-known, multinational corporations—Apple, GE, General Mills, Forbes, Google, and Microsoft to name a few—offer on-site classes to their employees, recognizing the business benefits when employees are grounded, calm, and focused. The United States Department of Veteran Affairs offers yoga at more than forty of its locations.

Kenneth began his yoga practice at a twice-weekly class sponsored by one of his employers, a national educational services firm where he was working part-time. At the same time, he was concluding a career as a school psychologist, and remembers that period of double-duty as "a particularly stressful time in my life." The pressure of the transition was eased by yoga, he says. He became more physically fit, tapped into the breathing practices to deal with stress, and developed close relationships with his new coworkers, who also were doing yoga.

"I was in far better shape to handle the demands of learning a new job, along with the familiar stress of working as a school psychologist—worry about troubled students, their parents, paperwork, and the repercussions of the law from unintended mistakes." He found yoga so useful he wanted to share it with others, and eventually began teaching at a downtown community center once a week.

The physical and mental benefits of a yoga practice have begun to generate a lot of attention. The Mayo Clinic website recommends yoga as a method of stress release, physical fitness, weight management, and managing chronic conditions, such as high blood pressure, cancer, depression, and insomnia. A 2004 Yale University School of Medicine study found that people who practiced yoga reduced their blood pressure, pulse, and risk of heart disease. A study published in a 2008 issue of *Journal of Alternative and Complementary Medicine* showed that military veterans with chronic low-back pain reported a significant reduction in pain, along with improvements in mood, energy, and quality of life.

This may explain why employers are becoming more eager to sponsor or subsidize yoga and meditation classes

for their employees. Who wouldn't want a healthier, energized workforce that is less stressed out and more focused?

Adam, who works in technical support for a large county
government, has taken advantage of the yoga classes offered
there and says both he and the workplace have benefited.
"Before I started yoga, I was exhausted from overwork and
felt underappreciated. Doing yoga helped relieve some of
the stress. Even though I still work in a less-than-hospitable
environment, I go back to work after yoga with a more centered and peaceful mindset."

Even the most stressful day is more tolerable since he
began taking yoga classes, agrees Adam's coworker, Savesh.
The physical practice makes him mindful about how he
treats his body at work, which he says gives him more energy and mental clarity. "I consciously adjust to a better
position with my neck/shoulders/back when I'm sitting at
the computer, and put my feet on the floor," Savesh says.
"I've noticed I feel less tired and sore at the end of the day
because of it."

METAPHORICALLY SPEAKING

While the physical and mental benefits of yoga include
increased energy, ability to deal with stress, and work satisfaction, the *asana* practice is also rich in metaphors for
the qualities needed to be successful at work: Intention.
Discipline and focus. Stability and strength. Flexibility.
Balance. Willingness to try something new.

The qualities that help you on the mat also serve
when you mindfully incorporate them into an off-the-mat
practice at work. Each quality has a role to play, and each
works in concert with the others—as always, integration

is key. Stability and strength are essential to achieving a yoga pose, focus is necessary to holding it, and without the cultivation of flexibility, the full expression won't be realized. Consistent, committed practice is essential to making progress, and that needs to be balanced with rest and energy renewal. Burning out on the altar of "getting ahead" does not ultimately benefit you or your workplace. Refilling your energy stores by keeping reasonable schedules and incorporating breaks does. The powerful combination of aspiration and perseverance spurs you toward excellence, but these qualities benefit from the counterpoise of letting go of the need for perfection and being attached to outcomes. The key is to develop the wisdom to know what serves you when.

On the mat, increasing effort and embracing the "edgy ache" that comes with moving deeper into a pose honors your practice and moves you further toward your potential. At work, if you can learn to hang with the discomfort of change rather than backing away, it can take you to wonderful places of discovery and creativity. Serving customers, colleagues, and other stakeholders is important, and a firm focus on the purpose of your work will help prevent you from unproductive contortions that don't really benefit the business you are in.

Just like on the mat, growth and improvement require consistent willingness to embrace the discomfort and disorientation that can accompany taking a leap—trying something new or going just a little bit further and deeper than you ever have before. To fully develop your potential, you need to stretch—taking on responsibilities that give you opportunities to grow. Strength and stability are foundational, but so is the flexibility to respond quickly to customer demands or a change in the marketplace.

Laura Karet, CEO of Giant Eagle, says she has learned to love falling out of a half-moon pose (*ardha chandrasana*) a challenging posture requiring strength, flexibility, and balance. "Yoga is wonderfully humbling. My practice is always reminding me that it's okay to make a mistake. It gives you the ability to accept yourself for who you are." That comes in handy in her leadership role, she says. "We have good days, and we have bad days. In order to be a good leader, you have to be okay with that. You fall down, but then you get up and try it again."

~~~~~~~

Five suggestions for practicing asana

1. Take a few minutes and jot down some of the literal and metaphorical gifts of an on-the-mat *asana* practice. What applications do you see that could transfer to the workplace?

2. If you have an asana practice, make a list of the benefits it has for you on the job.

3. For one week, commit to doing a physical yoga practice every day, whether it is a class or doing one sun salutation first thing in the morning. How does it make a difference in your day?

4. Make a list of yoga postures or stretches you can easily do at your desk. At times during your work day when you feel sluggish, stressed, or unfocused, take two minutes to do one or two of the stretches, then return to work. What do you notice?

5. Consider building a business case for your company sponsoring or subsidizing yoga classes at work. What benefits could you articulate to persuade employers it would be an asset to the enterprise you serve?

five

THE FOURTH LIMB: BREATH CONTROL (*PRANAYAMA*)

~~~~~~~~~~~~~~~~~~~~~~~~~~~~~~

*Listen, are you breathing just a little
and calling it a life?*

Mary Oliver

~~~~~~~~~~~~~~~~~~~~~~~~~~~~~~

Steve, a physician who works as a development officer for a large West Coast medical university, has found practicing breath control (*pranayama*) at work is a way to slow down a conversation, allowing him to be more grounded and thoughtful. When he is asked a question, he takes a slow, deep inhale and exhale before answering, a practice he adopted after a yoga teacher suggested it in class several years ago. "It helps me slow down that gerbil on the treadmill in my mind. I need that time to really think about what I have to say. It helps me not regret what I say."

He's noticed that most people at work answer questions without hesitation. It is not uncommon to hear someone respond before the other person even finishes a sentence. "I've even noticed in job interviews how quickly people respond," Steve says. "I ask questions, and a lot of times I get a canned response. It's like they came prepared with answers and are looking for a way to insert them into the conversation, instead of taking the time to really think about the question, then give a thoughtful response."

He's found the practice of deep breathing during interactions with others to be "positively disarming." Steve says that the *pranayama* shifts the energy on both sides of the conversation, allowing for more connection and deeper understanding.

Prana (energy or life force) and *ayama* (control) comprise yoga's Fourth Limb. You live because you breathe. Your breath fills you with the life force. *Pranayama* is about exploiting and harnessing that energetic force through attention to your breath.

A focus on breathing is an integral part of an on-the-mat practice and can definitely make a contribution to your work life as well. Thich Nhat Hanh says, "Breath is the bridge that connects life to consciousness, which unites your body to your thoughts." It is a preparation and foundational to effective meditation. Although you can learn all kinds of techniques associated with *pranayama*, the one thing you always have to do is be mindful of your breath.

When Jamie began doing yoga, he connected to the practice of *pranayama* right away. It is something he really enjoys doing during his on-the-mat practice—he visualizes, as well as feels, his breath as he moves through the postures and during the *pranayama* techniques Mary often incorporates into her classes. "When I try focusing on breath at work, that's another story," he says. "They say you write about or teach the things you need to learn yourself. That has been true for me as we've written this book."

Soon after our interview with Steve, Jamie was preparing for an interview with a *New York Times* reporter. He decided he was going to incorporate Steve's technique, inhaling and exhaling deeply before he responded to her questions. I was sitting in the room while he did the interview and noticed after about five minutes that he wasn't using the technique. Getting his attention, I mimed a big inhale and exhale. He nodded and tried the technique on the next question. But after a few minutes, he was back to answering immediately after the reporter's queries. After Jamie finished the interview, we talked about what got in the way of his staying connected to the *pranayama* technique. "I could feel myself wanting to show how competent I am by rushing in with the right answer. There was this little undercurrent of fear about allowing my breath to control the pace of the conversation." He was worried that if he hesitated, the reporter might think he was stumped or didn't know the answer. He didn't want the reporter to think she had picked the wrong guy to interview or that he was wasting her time. (Clearly she didn't, since several of his remarks were used in her piece.)

"The tape I have grown up with is that intelligence and decisiveness are connected, and pausing before answering might not seem to support either. During the interview, I was seeing the conversation as more important than how I showed up in the conversation," Jamie says. "And the other thing is that I just haven't developed a habit yet. It's something I'm going to continue working on. One of the benefits of yoga is the ongoing opportunity through practice to deal with this and other things in myself."

REDIRECTING ENERGY

Pranayama practice also is useful for helping you alter emotional and mental states that can get in the way of good work. Mindful breathing allows you to decelerate when you're feeling overwhelmed and stressed. It can calm an agitated or angry mind. When you're feeling lethargic and dull, mindful breathing techniques can help you restore energy.

When Zoe sees her first-graders' energy flagging, she gets them plugged back in to their schoolwork by using *pranayama* techniques. One of the kids' favorites is when she asks them to imagine they're in possession of a sword like Luke Skywalker's or Darth Vader's, and invites them to choose a color for their own blade.

"I tell them to close their left nostril, and then imagine that light sword going up their right nostril as they breathe in. Then I have them release their left nostril and plug their right, and imagine a different color coming out on the left as they exhale. I do a few rounds, right to left, left to right. Kids don't attach any judgment to doing it—they just think it is fun. It really is remarkable, because I can see their energy rev up almost immediately."

Next time you're feeling a little sleepy or sluggish, notice how you're breathing. When you're tired, breathing becomes shallow, allowing little fresh oxygen into your body. When you are feeling stressed, angry, or agitated, notice how choppy and uneven the breath is.

Lacey, who works as a police officer in Las Vegas, credits *pranayama* with her ability to stay focused and aware, even in the most extreme circumstances. She considers it a life-saving technique, and she isn't talking metaphorically. "When I am out on the shooting range, breath control allows me to have more accurate target practice. Your breath is a direct factor of the fluctuations of your mind. How you train is how you perform. This has been huge for me."

Huge is an understatement. She recalls one incident when she and her partner were forced from their patrol car after a gunman put several bullets into the door. They began to chase him down an alley as he continued to shoot at them. As Lacey ran, she was shouting into her radio, ordering backup help, and trying to direct other officers to their location. All the while the suspect continued to shoot. Then her gun jammed, and she started feeling panicky.

Lacey realized she was losing her breath. "You're already putting a strain on your cardiovascular system by running, and your sympathetic response has kicked into overdrive. I could observe that my breathing was becoming erratic, and I knew it was affecting my mental state. I had to slow it down if I wanted to do my job and not get killed."

As she ducked behind a wall to fix her gun, "I could actually see my mind running away from me." Lacey consciously decelerated her breath. "The training I have had in *pranayama* is invaluable in those situations, because I can get control of my breath quickly, which evens out my mind," she says. "Once I had my breath, I was able to quickly fix the gun, continue the chase, and get my shots off with precision."

PHYSICAL AND MENTAL BENEFITS

Studies show that slowing your breathing and other *pranayama* techniques can improve mood, mental alertness, and enhance memory—all qualities that will serve you at work. It is a physical practice that affects your cardiovascular system. Deep breathing circulates more oxygen through the body and into the brain. Slow, deep breathing can also help you find slumber more quickly and sleep more deeply. Better rest will leave you more refreshed and alert on the job.

Breathing also can be a means to find "the observer" that helps you recognize an emotional response before it gets in the way of what you want to accomplish. As you become aware of what your triggers are—conversations with your boss, a pushy colleague, having to give a presentation—*pranayama* gives you space to get grounded. With each breath, you can see yourself getting calmer and more able to focus. It doesn't take long. A dozen or so deep, mindful breaths won't cause you to miss any deadlines, yet can alleviate the anxiety and worry invoked by deadline pressure.

Visualization during *pranayama* is also effective, and something you can do at work without people even realizing it. As you close your eyes, imagine inhaling light into your lungs and gently expanding it out to your torso and limbs. Picture all the stress, negativity, and worry moving into your lungs as a gray mist, which will be expelled from your body on a deep exhale. The mist dissipates harmlessly into the atmosphere. Continue this breathing and visualization for several deep, even breaths, then open your eyes.

There. Doesn't that feel better?

Five suggestions for practicing pranayama

1. Make a mental note when you find yourself in high-stress situations, or when you're feeling tired or sluggish. How are you breathing? Jot down some notes about what you notice.

2. Experiment with altering your breathing patterns (suggested *pranayama* techniques are below) when you're in conversation, feeling stressed, or tired. What changes? How does it affect your conversations, relationships, or the dynamics at work?

3. For one day, experiment with taking one deep breath before responding to a statement or question. What do you notice? How does it change the quality of your responses? How does it affect the conversation?

4. Next time you're waiting for someone or standing in a long line, stand squarely on both feet, square your

shoulders, and focus on your breathing, or employ a *pranayama* technique. How does your experience change?

5. Try employing *nadi shodhana* in the evening and morning (see instructions on next page). What do you notice about your energy levels?

PRANAYAMA TECHNIQUES

Lion's Breath (Simhasana)

A wonderful way to eject tension, stress, frustration and anger from your body. This can be done standing, sitting, or kneeling.

1. Place your hands on your knees. Inhale through the nose.

2. Open your mouth wide and stick your tongue out as far as it will go, then exhale through the mouth, making a forecful "haaaaaaah" sound from the back of your throat.

3. Tilt your head slightly or bring your gaze toward the third eye as you exhale (optional).

4. Inhale, returning to a neutral face.

5. Repeat.

Alternate Nostril Breathing (Nadi Shodhana)

This simple technique is for balancing the mind and can be done by anyone (it even works on first-graders!). For calming, begin with the left nostril. For energizing, begin with the right. Start in a comfortable sitting position.

1. Using your right hand, fold your pointer and middle fingers into your palm, leaving your thumb, ring finger, and pinky sticking up (*Vishnu mudra*).

2. Use right thumb to close off right nostril.

3. Inhale slowly through left nostril, pause at the top of the inhale.

4. Close left nostril with ring finger and release thumb off right nostril.

5. Exhale through your right nostril.

6. Inhale through right nostril, pause at the top of the inhale.

7. Use right thumb, close right nostril, exhale through left nostril.

8. Inhale slowly through the left nostril, pause at the top. Close the left nostril with the ring finger, exhale through the right.

9. Block right nostril, exhale through left nostril.

10. Repeat for as many rounds as comfortable. Sit quietly for a few moments after you have dropped the techniques.

Cooling Breath (Sitali)

A perfect technique for hot weather or to use during a heated workout or practice. It cools the body, and is also said to aid with indigestion and hypertension.

1. Curl tongue into a tube (if your tongue does not curl, put the tip of your tongue behind the top of your front teeth).

2. Take a long, slow inhale (alternatively, take three "sips" of air on the inhale).

3. Close the mouth and slowly exhale through the nostrils. Repeat.

six

THE FIFTH LIMB: WITHDRAWAL OF THE SENSES (*PRATYAHARA*)

*The world within and the world without are
two entirely separate realities.
The external world dissipates energy,
but the internal world showers blessings
that fill the vacuum created by the world.*

Swami Rama

In the meditation hall, where hundreds of people sit in reflective silence, a woman begins to cry. The soft gulps of emotion soon escalate into deep, piercing sobs. The room begins to vibrate with bright tension as the outburst diverts others from their inward journeys, an unwitting and unwilling audience to the woman's sensational drama. After a few moments, the person assigned to "hold space" for those meditating quietly but firmly says, "Please. Be quiet."

Almost immediately, she is, and the room melts into silence.

Pratyahara combines the Sanskrit words *prati*, meaning against or away, and *ahara*, translated as food. This is a practice for gaining mastery over your senses and helps to develop the peaceful mind needed to achieve a deep, meditative state. Like the physical postures and breathing (*asana* and *pranayama*), it is a stepping stone. Many masters say that *pratyahara* is the most neglected limb of yoga, and yet it cannot be skipped on the way to meditation (*dhyana*) and absorption (*samadhi*). In the *Heart of Yoga*, T. K. V. Desikachar says *pratyahara* is when "our senses stop living off the things that stimulate." In Western society, it is a particularly challenging practice, since our environment has evolved into a state of perpetual sensory overload. David Frawley, founding director of the American Institute for Vedic Studies, says, "*Pratyahara* is the key between the outer and inner aspects of yoga. It shows us how to move from one to the other."

Computers, construction noise, food smells, televisions, billboards, beeping machines, music, traffic, overheard conversations—our senses are constantly assaulted.

Pico Iyer, author of *The Open Road: The Global Journey of the Fourteenth Dali Lama*, once told an interviewer, "I find that with my little laptop, I have the library of Alexandria and six billion people in my room. And it's very hard not to want to communicate with them and hear what they're saying and doing." And he does not even use social media! Ironically, the modern defense against chronic cacophony is to shove buds into our ear canals and blast in more noise. This might be an effective strategy for shutting out other surroundings, but it does nothing to train your mind to a more natural state of peace and calm. It is no wonder we are literally driven to distraction.

Frawley asserts that most people are unaware of what they are taking in through this constant barrage of stimulation and how it affects their mental state. He likens this "infobesity" as mindlessly feeding our psyches empty calories. Maintaining a healthy body requires exercise, sleep, and setting aside junk food for wholesome, natural sustenance. It is equally sensible to train the mind to be discriminating about the impressions you feed to your senses. "We accept impressions via the mass media that we would never allow in our personal lives," says Frawley. "We invite people into our houses through television and movies we would never allow into our homes in real life." All these images are imprinted onto your subconscious and play a part in making you who you are.

Pratyahara is a healthy and elegant antidote to sensual overcharging. The art of withdrawing sensation is difficult and requires a conscious effort to close off all your senses to the constant clamor of the world. The practice teaches you to direct your senses inward, like a turtle drawing into its protective shell, and it arrives through yogic practices such as breath control, intense focus, and meditation. With persistent practice, *pratyahara* helps you develop a natural mental force field that can protect your mind from the steady, stimulating diet of mental and sensual "junk food." It helps you get disentangled from the senses in a way that offers freedom. You become more calm and steady, less subject to the whims of emotion and attachment. "When the senses do not conform with their own objects but imitate the nature of the mind, that is *pratyahara*," say the Sutras.

Reining in sensation and turning inward is among the most difficult limbs to practice. The payoff is a calm, disciplined mind with the capacity for intense focus. The ability to instantly find respite from a hypercharged environment will aid you in developing self-awareness and managing your energy. It will lead to better work habits, decision-making, and leadership.

For all her adult life, ambition has fueled Emmalyn's career. She has been successful in the field of healthcare, where promotion after promotion eventually landed her a job as vice president of development for a medical research institute in northern California.

Emmalyn is responsible for raising millions of dollars for medical research, and she takes it seriously. She knows her work contribution helps make it possible for the institute to serve people who are suffering from serious diseases. The challenge in fundraising, which she calls a "lumpy business," is that instead of selling a tangible product, "We are transacting trust and faith and belief. I am trying to exert influence without control, which comes with a lot of pressure and stress." As her yoga practice has deepened over the last several years, she has begun to define success in different ways. "Within the last three years, I have realized that my yoga is a discipline for life. It has truly informed everything that I do, particularly at work. I'm far more observant of my own thoughts, which the practice of *pratyahara* helped me develop."

During one fundraising project, the practice helped stop a downward mental and emotional spiral when things weren't going as well as she hoped. At the end of a weekend event, she and her staff had achieved about 40 percent of the goal—much lower than expected. Emmalyn felt a sense of despair settling over the fundraising committee, and her anxiety ratcheted up. Her senses were agitated, and her head was whirling with a loop of questions for which no answers appeared: "Why aren't we meeting this goal? What did we do wrong? What more can we do?" She knew something had to change. At home that weekend, Emmalyn went to a quiet place to meditate and began to draw her senses inward, evoking calm and "the observer."

"What I observed clearly was my own franticness, which was a result of being overwhelmed with fear and desire. As I sat with that in meditation, I realized my motivating desire centered on showing people how competent I am. My fear was around potential failure, and how I might be judged if we didn't meet our goal." The loop of worrying about what could be or should be, and how people might view her performance, was obscuring her view of what was. "In fact, we were 41 percent toward the goal. We still had 10 days to achieve it." The observer asked: Are you *stressing* about the work, or are you actually *doing* the work? As she sat in silence, connected to breath, the answer Emmalyn was looking for emerged.

"In each new interaction with potential donors, I realized I had been dragging the baggage of all the previous phone calls where I didn't get what I wanted. I decided to ask myself: 'How am I going to be fully present on each new call?' Emmalyn set an intention to reach out to as many people as possible to help them understand the mission of the medical center and why support was needed—without fretting about the outcome. "Lo and behold, it happened! In a couple of days, we found a major gift that brought us 81 percent toward our goal. If my practice was not as strong as it is, I would have wallowed in the anxiety, or panicked, and I am absolutely certain I would have been less effective." This wasn't magic—it was the result of intentional action and focus combined with a determination to stay present.

SENSIBLE SENSES

Swami Shivananda compares the senses to children, because without training, their actions are instinctual and unruly. Surrendering our minds to sensory overload is the equivalent of giving children a constant diet of sweets and caffeinated drinks. (Our son-in-law, Christopher, likes to say, "In goes the sugar, out comes the crazy.") If your mind is connected to a feeding tube of mental junk, how can it stay sharp, aware, and attentive? The more sensations you are bombarded with, the more stimulation and excitement you crave—it is all too easy to become addicted. This leaves you in a state of being constantly wired while simultaneously skating on the edge of exhaustion.

Just as children need boundaries and guidance to become calm, disciplined, and well-behaved, the mind can benefit from training and setting limitations. This doesn't require you to completely remove yourself from the environment—it would be hard to get work done from a cave!

Nor is the goal to constantly suppress your senses or your mind. It is, however, possible to gain mental mastery so that the external senses don't always rule your thoughts and actions.

Our teacher, Mary Bruce, travels with the country-rock band Sugarland. Her role is to lead the musicians and crew through a yoga practice before each show. In the summer of 2011, Mary and the band were waiting in an underground bunker that led to the stage moments before a show was scheduled to begin in Indianapolis. Just as they were forming their customary pre-show prayer circle, they heard the crowd's cheers devolve into a burst of panicked screaming. A micro-instant later, Mary and the others were knocked down by a thunderous impact. The bunker turned dark, accompanied by an ominous soundtrack of hysterical screams and cries for help. "We knew the set had collapsed, but that's all," Mary recalls. "We had no idea what was going on. We just knew it was bad." The exits from the bunker were blocked, and the group was terrified the bunker would collapse on top of them. "We couldn't get out. We all ran to a corner and huddled together."

INSTINCTUAL MINDFULNESS

Due to her years of intensive yoga training, Mary's response was instinctual. "I stayed with my breath the entire time, and immediately began reciting a mantra" she says. This helped lead her to *pratyahara*, erecting a mental barrier against the frightening sensations. She was able to access the state described by Desikachar where "the links between mind, senses, and external objects that have nothing to do with the breath are cut." She stayed with her silent mantra as the lights flickered on, and she helped others stay calm.

Then they waited. For 45 minutes they waited, until at last the emergency crew managed to unblock an entrance and free them. It seemed miraculous that no one in the bunker had been seriously injured.

It wasn't until Mary got back to her hotel room that the full realization of what had happened became clear. Watching a television news report, she learned a fierce gust of wind had lifted and then blown over scaffolding, sound equipment, and the set, which crashed onto the stage as it collapsed. The accident killed seven spectators and injured many others. If Mary and the band had been on stage even five seconds earlier, they surely would have died.

Throughout the traumatic events, yoga helped Mary tune in to herself and stay present. "The whole time, I stayed centered, observing, participating, but not reactionary. When I finally saw it on TV, it shocked me. It wasn't really until then that I felt it in my physical body."

Pratyahara has also been a crucial work tool for Gina, who is constantly confronted with life-and-death decisions while working as a physician's assistant in hospital emergency rooms. She has found *pratyahara*, which she learned about in her yoga training, to be invaluable in serving patients. "On average, healthcare providers in the ER are interrupted once every six minutes. And even when we are not being interrupted, a din of activity is going on all around us. In that environment, it can be very hard to concentrate on the details of a patient's situation, analyze test results, and make solid, educated decisions on the best course of care."

Gina's job requires her to efficiently integrate information from patients, their families, nurses, technicians, and specialists to make decisions that have serious, life-altering consequences. Overlooking minor details can be disastrous. *Pratyahara* helps her filter out the unneeded sensations that distract from a laser focus on patients' needs.

"I have to let go of the strange smells, the sounds, and the close confines of my work space," Gina says. "I dial down my senses and find that place inside that allows me to focus from a clear and peaceful place so I can make smart and safe decisions. One patient at a time."

Five suggestions for practicing pratyahara

1. Identify and list the people or places at work where drama, over-stimulation, and/or boundary issues "hook" you. What sensations do you experience? Can you minimize contact with these situations? If not, visualize "unhooking" or "unplugging" yourself when you're in those circumstances. Notice what changes for you.

2. Do a technology fast. Commit to a time where phones are turned off, computers unplugged, television screens are blank. Set aside newspapers and magazines. If you can't manage a full day in the beginning, start with an hour, and work your way up.

3. Practice withdrawing unwelcome impressions from your mind. When you imagine failure, skip the thought away, like a pebble on a lake. Are you mentally reenacting arguments with your boss or a coworker? Close your eyes, focus on breath, and reconnect to the present moment.

4. Attend a silent retreat, or create your own by spending the day alone in a natural setting or quiet sanctuary,

soaking in the quiet. Train your mind by noticing just one thing: the blue sky, the clouds, leaves on a tree, pebbles in a stream. Do you find yourself bored and restless? Can you hang with the discomfort? If your mind can't turn off, try using *pranayama* to settle it.

5. Instead of just drifting off to sleep, shut down your senses, one at a time, as you lie in bed. Close your eyes. Notice the ambient sounds, and then withdraw your hearing. What can you smell? Take it in, then let it go. Feel the sensation of your body on the mattress, your head on the pillow. Bring the sensations inward, one body part at a time.

seven

THE SIXTH LIMB: FOCUS (*DHARANA*)

~~~~~~~~~~~~~~~~~~~~~~~~~~~~~~~~~~~

Settle in the here and now.
Reach down into the center
where the world is not spinning
and drink this holy peace. . . .

Donna Faulds

~~~~~~~~~~~~~~~~~~~~~~~~~~~~~~~~~~~

M ary was in a room filled with more than sixty yogis, though she might as well have been alone. When she is on her mat, Mary says there is nothing else: "It is me, my mat, and my breath. I am so focused on my practice that I don't even realize who is on either side of me. After class is over, I look around and think, 'Oh yeah, there is so and so.'"

In this class, her longtime teacher, Rod Stryker, was talking the yogis through the mechanics of Lord of the Dance pose, *natarajasana*, an advanced posture requiring great strength, flexibility, and most especially, balance. On the mat next to Mary, a friend wobbled, fell out of the pose, then executed a tuck, tumble, and roll right under Mary's feet.

Her pose never wavered.

❧

Focus, or *dharana*, is the sixth limb of yoga. This practice is devoted to bringing a laser-like concentration to one thing—a mantra, the flicker of candlelight, a mental image, or a spot on the wall. This state of deep concentration, when mastered, forces the mind into the now. It is fully present in this place, at this time.

We train to develop our muscles and our memory, and fill our minds with knowledge, skills, and experience. *Dharana* is something different. It is training the mind itself to gain mastery over what it pays attention to (and how that attention is paid) as a way of staying present.

The mental exercise begins by focusing on an object and developing the discipline to return to it every time the mind fluctuates. When you begin a *dharana* practice, you'll likely notice you have a very chatty mind. And it's not so easy to command silence. Michael Singer, author of *The Untethered Soul: The Journey Beyond Yourself*, writes about this in the first few pages of his book:

> *In case you haven't noticed, you have a mental dialogue going on inside your head that never stops. It just keeps going and going. . . . Why do you even tolerate that voice talking to you all of the time? Even when it is saying something soothing and nice, it is still disturbing every-thing you are doing. If you spend some time observing this mental voice, the first thing you will notice is that it never shuts up. When left to its own, it just talks.*

Think about it—one of the lines that divides what is considered sane and insane is often nothing more than verbalization. Imagine if you gave voice to every thought in your head. People would think you were mad! Yet all day long, you are listening to the voices that are constantly chattering away inside the mind, and you probably think they are "you." Singer's book points out how irrelevant those voices are. They are a major distraction from the now. In reality, neither past nor future exist except as memories our brain has stored (and likely altered) or in the imagin-ing of an unknowable future. Even so, that voice is con-vincing—you think it is you, and you believe, react, and respond to what it says. It evokes emotion. It creates energy. But it is not you—and if you train your mind to become the observer, it will help you see what is *really* happening.

The late Steve Jobs, the much-lauded genius behind Apple, was a Zen Buddhist with a committed meditation practice. In his biography authored by Walter Isaacson, Jobs says that with focus, the mind makes room "to hear more subtle things. That's when your intuition starts to blossom and you start to see things more clearly. . . . Your mind just slows down, and you see a tremendous expanse in the moment. You see so much more than you could see before."

Dharana practice is devoted to instructing your mind to stop drifting back to what happened yesterday, mulling over today's to-do list, or projecting what might happen tomorrow. *Dharana* prepares the mind to quickly drop into deep meditation, and develops your ability to steady the mental fluctuations that can keep you distracted, unhappy, and divorced from the present. When you can control your mind, you will see the power of now as everything else dissolves away.

ACCIDENTAL *DHARANA*

Have you ever been so absorbed and passionate about a task or a project that you worked for hours without realizing the hours had passed? Practicing *dharana* will help you call on that state of steady, calm, focused concentration at will.

Your mind's predilection to wander is easy to see in an on-the-mat practice, especially as a beginner. I have attempted balancing poses, both simple and complex, hundreds of times in yoga class. I nail it, seconds pass, and from my peripheral vision I notice the person in front of me begin to waver and wobble. As I see my neighbor fall out of the pose, my balance suddenly becomes precarious, then impossible to hold. It is much easier for me to maintain balancing poses during home practice, when my mind has only my body to focus on.

During balancing poses, yoga teachers recommend finding a spot for your *drishti*, or gaze, and keeping it there to help you retain balance. Focusing intently—on a spot on the wall, the floor, the mat in front of you—allows your mind to rivet on to one thing, helping the body maintain balance. This was a light bulb moment for me—balancing has less to do with my body's ability and much more to do with my mental state.

Patanjali says, "Disease, dullness, doubt, carelessness, laziness, worldly-mindedness, illusion, missing the point, instability—these are obstacles in Yoga." These also describe the obstacles to good work, and *dharana* can help you conquer them!

THE MYTH OF MULTITASKING

At work one day, I found myself sucked in to a huge argument about the importance of multitasking. It was being extolled as a virtue by an editor who was coaching a young reporter. Overhearing the conversation, the science reporter piped up, asserting that multitasking was impossible. Several of my coworkers, who fancied themselves expert and efficient multitaskers, vociferously argued that she was wrong. I was on the fence. I contended that it might be possible, but wasn't necessarily desirable.

The next day, the science reporter produced research data to back up her argument, including studies that reveal multitasking is actually an illusion produced by the efficiency of our amazing brains. The human brain is so proficient and speedy at jumping from one thought to another that we're convinced we really are able to do several things at once. But that cranial capacity for firing quickly just allows us to delude ourselves, and the research shows it exacts a price.

Scientists have used advanced brain scanning technology to see what happens when we try to do more than one thing at a time. One article we read likened the brain's functioning to the frenzied mental state of an inexpert plate spinner. If this brain pattern is continually reinforced, the ability to concentrate eventually is damaged, and the quality of your work is diminished, according to research conducted at MIT.

Glenn Wilson, a psychiatrist at the University of London, reported that even *thinking* about multitasking can cause a brain bottleneck. Doing two things that employ the same parts of your brain, such as talking on the phone while writing an email, can produce the same foggy state as losing a night's sleep, and knock a whole ten points from your IQ, according to his study.

Dharana is a natural remedy to this modern multitasking madness. Developing the ability to employ this kind of concentration at work seems like a no-brainer, if you will excuse the pun. Imagine if you had the ability to fixate on the needs of the customer or the students in front of you. What if you could summon, at will, total focus on the report that needs to be written, the conversations at meetings, or assembling a machine? Surely that would have an impact on the quality of your work.

Perhaps you are thinking, "I can't do that! The distractions at work make it impossible!" Phones are blaring, beeping, or (even on "silent mode") buzzing. Your neighbors are yakkety-yakking, and the siren smell of coffee in the break room tempts. Your email inbox is overflowing, your meetings are stacked up, and the project files on your desk are towering. And every time you sit down swearing to accomplish *something*, inevitably someone interrupts with a request. And you're supposed to focus?

That's where a *dharana* practice can help. One of the miracles of your mind is that it is malleable, trainable. Just as your muscles can be developed to support you in the most challenging of poses, so can your mind be developed to focus like a laser on what is in front of you right now. Neurons can be trained to fire differently, to carve out new pathways in the brain.

FENCING YOURSELF OFF FOR FOCUS

At the last newspaper where I worked as an editor, managers typically left the doors to their offices open. It was rare to see doors closed unless someone was out of the office, a meeting was being held, or a performance review going on. The "open door" culture made a statement about managers being available if needed, but also invited mindless interruptions.

During the last several months of my job there, I worked for a woman who had established a different sort of routine. She would check in with her staff first thing in the morning, and then seclude herself, office door closed, while she took care of tasks that needed to be done. Because she was flouting office culture, some of my coworkers muttered about her being standoffish.

That wasn't my experience. I found her to be warm, caring, and personable. She frequently checked in with people, and if you really needed an answer, she made herself accessible. My feelings about her leaned more toward envy. I admired willingness to signal that it was her time to concentrate, which minimized the constant interruptions an open door solicited. Although I didn't hesitate to knock if something was urgent, her closed door also made me realize there were many decisions I could make on my own, or that could wait until she wrapped up and opened the door.

Of course, boundaries are harder to create if you're working in a cubicle or open office environment—no door to close! However, other distraction-busting strategies can be developed. When work requires *dharana*, post a sign in a prominent space around your desk saying "Do Not Disturb. On Deadline." If your work environment allows it, alert key coworkers that you're moving to a quieter location so that you can better focus on something that needs to get done. I've known people who would arrange their schedules, if feasible, to carve out hours in the morning or evening when coworkers would not be around so they could work with fewer distractions. Or if your employer is flexible, build a business case for working at home.

Unless you are a hermit, external distractions are almost impossible to avoid. Even if you work at home, things are bound to clamor for your attention (the laundry, the cat, the refrigerator). Training your mind to make everything but the present moment recede from consciousness can be invaluable for managing those distractions.

ADMIT YOU ARE OUT OF CONTROL

Another way to develop *dharana* at work is by listening. How often do you zone in and out of conversations at work, even in important meetings? How many times do you use your mental faculties to start formulating an argument to what the person is saying, instead of trying to understand what is being said? A good *dharana* practice would be to listen intently, even if you think you have heard it before, or you disagree, or it provokes an emotional response. Make a game of it—listen so closely you'd be able to repeat what they had to say word for word. In our *Authentic Conversations* work, we advocate that people "argue the other person's side" as a way of creating understanding and letting the other person know they have been truly heard. It doesn't require agreement, it just means demonstrating that you get their point of view. Without an intentional focus on what they are saying, it's not possible to do.

Practicing *dharana* will increase understanding and improve the quality of your relationships with coworkers and customers. It will enhance your ability to work with others collaboratively, cohesively, and efficiently.

THE PRESENT IS A GIFT

Dharana demands presence. You cannot do quality work if your mind is chattering away, reminding you about picking up the kids from school later, or percolating on where you're going to meet your friends after work, or fretting about tomorrow's doctor appointment. The time to focus on picking up the children from school is when you are picking them up, not when you're at your desk crafting an email that will update your coworkers on an important project.

Dharana also helps you detach from desire—to get your way, to win the argument, to distract yourself from a work deadline. The clamor of competing priorities is held at bay. Decide what most deserves your focus, right now, and give it all your attention. Move on to the next, and repeat.

Five suggestions for practicing dharana

1. Start small. Sit in a quiet room and focus on a physical object—a photo, a piece of art, a candle flame. See if you can "see" the object without thinking for three minutes. Increase by a few minutes each day.

2. Swami Kriyananda suggests it is more powerful to think positively about one thing than avoid thinking about many things. Decide what will get your attention for a predetermined length of time. Then list the things that might be a distraction. Make a mental note of when you will give yourself time to think of those things before beginning your task.

3. Close your door, turn off your phone, shut down the Internet—eliminate any potential distractions and commit to total attention on one task for at least thirty minutes. Set a timer. When it goes off, see what you notice about your mind, and what has been accomplished.

4. During meetings, listen closely to everything that is said, without judging what is said. Stay present to the conversation by being silent, unless your input/feedback is requested. After the meeting, see how much of the conversation you can capture in notes.

5. When you are feeling tired or frustrated by a task, "take five." Focusing on the sound of your breath, or the rise and fall of your belly, take five full, deep breaths. Then reassess. If you're still feeling frazzled, maybe it's time to conclude. If you're feeling better, try five more pages, or five more emails, then do the breathing technique once again.

eight

THE SEVENTH LIMB: MEDITATION (*DHYANA*)

〰〰〰〰〰〰〰〰〰〰〰

If we know the divine art of concentration,
if we know the divine art of meditation,
if we know the divine art of contemplation,
easily and consciously we can unite the inner world
and the outer world.

Sri Chinmoy

〰〰〰〰〰〰〰〰〰〰〰

B efore meeting with potential donors, Steve spends a few minutes in meditation, concluding with an intention that helps him connect to purpose:

May [this person] be happy and peaceful
May she be free from all inner and outer harm
May her mind and body be healthy
May she be happy with things as they are
May she live with the ease of well-being

Steve, the physician/fundraiser at a major west coast university medical center, is charged with raising money to support the goals of the institution—at least on paper. But he likes to turn that description on its head. He considers himself an advocate for donors and in service to connecting the donors' passions and motivations to the needs of the institution.

One of the things meditation practice does for him is remind him that the focus of his work is not the transaction, but building relationships. "When I am able to quiet myself and turn my focus toward understanding and advocating for the donor, I know I am not going to take actions that are coercive or manipulative. The meditation has been a way to bring the potential donor to the front of my mind. I can think about their needs instead of 'How do I get them to do something I want them to do?' Using manipulative selling techniques may get you something in the moment, but it won't get you a lasting relationship."

Relationships are key in his line of work, and Steve says that being intentional about donor advocacy has brought long-term gains he is convinced he wouldn't have otherwise seen. "Through service to others, we really do get what we need," Steve says. "After six years, I am beginning to see how fruitful those trusted relationships can be. People know my intention, and they trust me. In the last three months, two donors have called me and said, 'I think I could do something better.' That is fantastic, and so satisfying."

One of the purposes of meditation is to remove attention from your body, the environment, and the passage of time, says Joe Dispenza, author of *Breaking the Habit of Being Yourself*. "What you intend, what you think, becomes your focus instead of these externals. The practice also is a means for you to move beyond your linear, analytical mind so that you can access the subconscious, where your habits reside."

Eknath Easwaran calls meditation a "skill for living," with benefits that can be drawn upon at any time, in any place. The benefits of meditation (*dhyana*) are backed up by empirical data. Of the eight limbs, meditation has been the most scrutinized by researchers. Technological advances have even been able to show its effects on the brain. Findings from some of these research studies include:

~ Herbert Benson, a researcher at Harvard, discovered that meditation could slow the respiratory rate and oxygen consumption, lower heart rates, and reduce elevated blood pressure. Several studies have since built on his work.

~ Researchers using imaging technology have found that people develop measurable changes in the brain associated with compassion, self-awareness, and memory after learning "mindfulness meditation," which involves periods of intense focus and concentration.

~ The research of Dr. Sat Bir Khalsa, a Harvard scientist who works with the Kripalu Institute for Extraordinary Living on yoga-related research, showed in 2009 that yoga and meditation lessens anger, depression, and performance anxiety in young musicians.

~ Even short-term meditation improves self-control, mood, stress response, and immunity response, suggests the research done in 2007 by Dr. Michael Posner, University of Oregon, and Dr. Yi-Yuan Tang, Texas Tech University.

~ Actual alterations in brain structure underlie the cognitive and psychological benefits reported by people who meditate, according to a study led by Harvard-affiliated researchers at Massachusetts General Hospital. Sara Lazar, senior author of the study, says research shows that meditation's benefits come from more than just spending time relaxing.

Easwaran warns that is important to distinguish true meditation from other like-minded pursuits, such as taking it easy or napping. In *Conquest of Mind*, he writes that meditation-like techniques "may be inspiring, they may be good for your physical health, but as far as accomplishing enduring beneficial changes in the mind, they have no more effect than writing on water."

MEDITATION'S WORKPLACE BENEFITS

Major corporations such as Apple, HBO, General Mills, Nike, Prentice Hall Publishing, and Proctor & Gamble are so sold on the benefits of *dhyana* that they have found ways to bring meditation into the workplace. These employers have instituted practices such as encouraging workers to take time for the practice, creating meditation spaces, and providing training. Google offers its employees a seven-week training course in mindfulness meditation. It's taught by engineer Chade-Meng Tan, whose official title is Jolly Good Fellow. He's written a book, *Search Inside Yourself: The Unexpected Path to Achieving Success, Happiness (and World Peace)*, and created an open-source training program for other companies.

The Jolly Good Fellow says meditation builds emotional intelligence, which helps people be more effective at work—and that provides a bonus to the bottom line.

Oprah Winfrey, who did a story on Transcendental Meditation that aired in 2012, was inspired to incorporate the practice into her work day. TM, as it is known, typically involves two 20-minute sessions daily of meditating with a mantra. Winfrey and seven colleagues began stopping their work at 9 A.M. and again at 4:30 P.M. for meditation, no matter what was going on. During an interview, she told Dr. Mehmet Oz that her little group of seven became 70 people and kept growing until it was 270. Now everyone in the company practices *dhyana*.

The benefits have been remarkable, she told Oz. "You can't imagine what has happened in the company. People who used to have migraines, don't. People are sleeping better. People have better relationships. People interact with other people better. It's been fantastic."

At a nationally known wellness and learning spa, meditation became the deciding factor in the decision to hire someone for a key management position in technology. "We had a pool of great candidates and had narrowed it down to three people," says Maya, the human resources director. "It was an important hire. This person would be running a department that was somewhat troubled, and we knew it could be a rocky road for whoever stepped in. All the candidates told us they were undaunted by that, and all were highly qualified and had similar education and work experience."

In the end, the job went to the candidate who had a longtime yoga and meditation practice. "That is what swayed us to hire him over the others," Maya says. "We thought with the stress and challenge of this job, he would be more equipped to handle the challenges. And so far, it has proven to be a great decision. He is cool as a cucumber, always smiling and serene. And he has made a big impact in a short time."

A SOLO PRACTICE

For people who work in places that don't encourage—much less provide time for—periods of reflection, meditation at work might seem unrealistic. Imagine your boss finding you in your office as you practice *dhyana*, eyes closed, body still, senses withdrawn. When asked what you are doing, you reply, "I am trying not to think." You're more likely to get an "outta here" than an "atta boy."

Meditation practice, however, doesn't have to take big chunks of time out of your day. You can even do it at work without anyone knowing. Our friend and colleague Noah Blumenthal, author of *Be the Hero: Three Powerful Ways to Overcome Challenges in Work and Life*, has developed a simple meditation that he practices throughout the day, three seconds at a time. He developed it after "I had a far less than patient moment with my daughter and wished never to lose my cool with her again." Many of his executive coaching clients have adopted the technique with great success, and he shared it with us at an author retreat. Blumenthal says, "It has been transformational for me and almost everyone I have introduced it to."

The meditation has five parts, which take just a few seconds:

1. Deep inhale through the nose.
2. Body scan for stress, consciously trying to relax any places where you hold tension.
3. Say your focus word or intention (be present, compassion, focus, energy, patience, relax, etc.).
4. Release your breath, again through the nose.
5. Smile.

The technique is based on neuroscience, an interest of Blumenthal's, and the idea is to connect a desired behavior—patience in his case—with breathing, body awareness, and a positive mood. (Hence, the smile.) Breathing through the nose is important, because the nasal passages are smaller than the mouth and will naturally slow your breathing. Your breath rate influences heart rate, and a slower heart rate is a key predictor of health benefits around stress. He does this technique 20 to 30 times a day without anyone noticing by using a phone app that gives him an unobtrusive signal every fifteen minutes. The power is in the repetition, because every time you repeat the practice, neurons are being fired that eventually will rewire your brain.

Just developing a robust meditation practice at home will have benefits that stay with you at work. It isn't as difficult as you might think, and it doesn't require sitting for hours in lotus pose. Even a few minutes of daily meditation has been shown to be beneficial for stress relief and mental clarity that last well beyond the time actually spent meditating.

At the office, taking a few quiet moments—like Steve does before his meetings—is a small time investment that reaps a big payoff. This brief disconnection from thinking about work will actually help you work more effectively. The practice will help you become more grounded and calm, and clarify your intentions and focus about what you can accomplish at work that best serves the enterprise.

Many formal programs are available that teach you to meditate, and most yoga studios and retreat centers offer meditation classes. In addition, myriad books have been written that include instructions on how to develop a *dhyana* practice and extol the benefits of meditation on your mind, health, and relationships. (We list some of our favorites in the Resources section of this book.) But the most essential quality in developing a meditation practice is the willingness to commit. A quiet time, a reflective space, every day.

"*Dhyana* is a place where action and insight become one," write Rolf Gates and Katrina Kenison in *Meditations from the Mat.* "When we are in this state of sustained focus and flow, the actions of attention and the insight gained from detached observation occur simultaneously. Here, in this timeless still point, we grow up."

Five suggestions for practicing dhyana

1. You don't have to sit for hours in lotus pose for meditation to be effective. Start with three to five minutes a day for one week. Close your eyes and focus on breath. Feel the air in your nostrils, or notice your belly or chest rising and falling. To help still your mind, try a simple mantra such as *so hum* ("I am that," with *so* on the inhale, *hum* on the exhale). After a week, what do you notice?

2. Before a meeting, carve out two to three minutes where you can sit quietly and reflect on your intentions. What do you want to create in the moment? How do you want to bring yourself present? You might want to try doing the same thing together with team members or a client before starting a project.

3. Consider starting meetings with a brief period of silence and focus on breath. If your team or coworkers are reluctant, mention the research, and ask them to experiment with the practice for a week. What changes?

4. Note the times you find it hard to focus on your work or feel unmotivated. If possible, find a quiet place where you can disconnect, meditate, or do breathing (*pranayama*). Then return to work. How does the practice affect your focus?

5. Consider choosing a theme or intention for your meditation time: gratitude, courage, well-being, compassion, forgiveness, truth. Stick with the topic for a set period of time. Journal about insights and discoveries that reveal themselves.

nine

THE EIGHTH LIMB: ABSORPTION (*SAMADHI*)

One is rigorously awakened by
stirring the desire for enlightenment itself.

Dogen Zenji

You can hear the smile in Heather's voice as she talks about the day she took her father to his first yoga class. She is a senior manager at a wellness resort in the southwestern United States. At one time, her father had been an elite runner who placed in the Boston marathon. As a runner, her father had always been attentive to the warm-up, cool-down stretching that athletes do. Aging eventually slowed him down, and some of the activities that once had fueled his passion became unavailable to him. Heather's sporadic attempts to get him interested in yoga had gone nowhere until he was in his eighties. While he was visiting from the East Coast, she finally persuaded him to come to the resort and take a yoga class with her.

"Our mission here [at the wellness resort] is intended to be holistic. What we do has a spiritual aspect that is centered on mindfulness and living your life in a fully present way. So many times I had tried to explain to my dad what mindfulness is, and why it is important to me, but he just wasn't interested," Heather says. "On the way to the yoga class, I was trying again to make him understand the shift that happens when you are truly present. But it didn't seem to resonate or even interest him. He was looking out the window, saying, 'Uh huh . . . Uh huh.'"

It turned out that Heather and her father were the only two people in the yoga class that day, which meant the teacher could lavish abundant attention on her father. Being athletic and competitive, her father was pleased to discover that he was good at yoga. He moved from pose to pose with deep concentration, going inward with an intensity that Heather hadn't seen for a long time.

When the instructor brought them out of *savasana*, her father looked at Heather and said, "What's the deal? We're done? You don't think I am capable of doing a 90-minute class?"

"It *was* a 90-minute class, Dad," Heather said. "We have been doing yoga for 90 minutes."

Her father looked skeptical and, after a glance at the clock, surprised. "I was in the zone, I guess," he said. "Everything else just fell away. It feels to me like hardly any time has passed at all."

"This is what I have been trying to explain to you," Heather told her father. "You experienced mindfulness. You were fully present."

Her father continued to practice yoga until his death a few years later.

———

Yoga's eight limbs are like a flower bud. As each layer of petals opens, it reveals the next, and the next, until the fragrant core of full blossoming is revealed. At the peak of its bloom, the flower is fully realized. *Samadhi* is self-realization, the full bloom of yoga. All the limbs of yoga are designed to lead you to *samadhi*.

The Shabhala Dictionary of Buddhism and Zen describes the Eighth Limb as "a non-dualistic state of consciousness." The Sanskrit translation of *samadhi* means "to bring together, to merge." In the Sutras, it is described as uniting oneself or being absorbed into a collective consciousness or the divine. In this flowering, the Self unites with the Ultimate Reality. Ego disappears. In modern language, you might describe this as being "in the zone." Reality shifts.

In her memoir *Eat, Pray, Love*, Elizabeth Gilbert described the experience like this: "Time gets all screwy in this thunderous space, and I am taken—numbed, dumbed, and stunned—to all sorts of worlds, and I experience every intensity of sensation."

The Sutras and various yoga masters describe up to four different states of *samadhi*, the highest of which is described by the Maharishi Mahesh Yogi as "a state which you cannot describe." While all that might sound a little wild for the world of work, it is not as bizarre as it might seem. Pandit Rajmani Tigunait points out that "The art of living in the world can be mastered without ignoring the supreme goal of life. When we achieve this mastery while retaining our spiritual focus, we achieve a state of balance and harmony, disregarding neither worldly obligations nor spiritual needs."

Mihaly Csikszentmihalyi, a renowned researcher in the area of happiness and creativity, has written extensively about a state he describes as "flow," which has the same qualities as those attributed to *samadhi*. He says the key to achieving this state is developing the ability to "control the contents of our consciousness." This is what ultimately allows people to determine the quality of their lives. His research supports the notion that achieving this state in a work setting is not uncommon, and he asserts that the best place to have this sort of experience is while we are doing meaningful work. When work offers high-challenge, high-skill opportunities, it engenders feelings of concentration, creativity, and satisfaction "flow." In this situation, he says, "Your sense of time disappears. You forget yourself. You feel a part of something larger."

Some of the practices that lead you toward *samadhi*—particularly *pratyahara, dharana, dhyana*—might seem antithetical to the workplace. It's probably hard to imagine an on-the-job scenario where you are encouraged to withdraw your senses, spend time in a dimly lit room looking inward, or silently chant a mantra while sitting at your desk with your eyes closed. Even so, if you were to achieve *samadhi* in the course of your work, it would look like dedication, creativity, and commitment. You would be consistently energized, enthusiastic, productive, and content. You would be, as they say, "absorbed by your work."

Yet *samadhi* is more than just losing track of time or becoming unaware of your surroundings for a time. Zoning out at a meeting, for instance, could be a sign of boredom or an untrained mind. You might get lost working on a project to the point that time flies, but that may just speak to an ability to focus intently. *Samadhi* is more than that, because it is accompanied by a shift in consciousness. "Whether we are experiencing *samadhi* or not is not shown by sitting cross-legged with closed eyes and a meaningful expression on our face," says T. K. V. Desikachar. "We know we are experiencing *samadhi* if we can see and understand things that we could not see or understand before."

Brynne, a healthcare professional who has practiced yoga for nearly a decade, remembers having such a shift in an unlikely "union" with a difficult woman that forever altered the way she attends to patients. She is a physician's assistant, and was working in a public health clinic when she walked into an examination room and had a visceral negative reaction to the obese and unkempt woman she saw.

"When you walk into an examination room, you get an immediate first impression. Usually the first thought is 'sick' or 'not sick.' My first impression was, 'Whoa. This is not a beautiful individual.'" The woman was surrounded by several concerned family members, but she didn't seem to have symptoms that needed immediate attention. What she mostly had was a bucketful of complaints. Even in a medical setting, Brynne knows that not everyone you see is obviously sick, "but you still have to figure out a way to help them."

As the patient let loose her litany of gripes, Brynne was awash in judgment about the woman's sharp tone, edgy demeanor, and annoying mannerisms. But what really got her attention was the woman's out-of-control anger. She could feel herself tensing up in a way she knew would not be useful. For the briefest of moments, Brynne closed her eyes and connected to her breath. Inhale, exhale. In that moment, she felt the shift. "It was almost like I disappeared. I imagined that woman as me. She was me. Her face was mine. Her body, her family—all mine. Even her anger was mine." The judgment about the patient's looks, her mannerisms, and anger dissipated as Brynne became totally absorbed in helping this woman. The experience took on a surreal quality, as though she was attending to herself.

"We ended up having an amazing conversation. After a while, she calmed down, and I consulted with a psychologist. We sent her home with medicine and a referral for counseling. After she was gone, I realized I had actually lost myself to helping her, and I also knew without a doubt that I *had* helped her. You know, it is so easy to feel separate from patients. You see yourself as the expert. After that, I realized how often I was having these internal conversations: 'I would never be like them. I would never make those unhealthy decisions. I would never be so weak to complain about something like that.'"

Because of the experience of absorption with that patient, her thinking shifted in a profound way. Brynne realized she was connected to everyone. *She was everyone.* "The people you want to disconnect from are the ones who probably need you the most. I have never looked at patients the same way after that day."

THE POINT OF YOGA IS *SAMADHI*

It is all too easy to fall into the trap of letting someone else define your purpose at work. You are bombarded with myriad external messages that reinforce the assumption that someone else is responsible for what happens in the workplace. You're hired for your skills and experience, but then you're told what to do and when to do it. If you do it reliably and reasonably well, you get compensation. In that transaction, something often gets lost. It is easy to lose sight of who you want to be and what you want to create. If you can discover that, and bring it to work with you, it becomes liberating, according to my friend and mentor Barclay Hudson. He says, "It's not just the practice of yoga, but the practice of mindful work—work as satisfaction in itself—that yields practice for everything else in life. Work liberation is practice for liberation of life, practice at being fully alive."

The truth is, only one person is capable of defining your purpose, and that person can only be found by looking into a mirror. Through a dedicated practice of the Eight Limbs of Yoga, your *dharma*, or life's purpose, becomes clearer. And when it does, the way you live it out is energized by awareness and aligned action. Understanding your purpose is the greatest contribution you can make to yourself, those you work with, and the enterprise in which you make a contribution.

If you are clear about purpose, it is easier to find that "sense of union" at work, a kind of joy that is felt whether you are sweeping a floor, serving a customer, developing computer code, running a company, or doing brain surgery. In those moments, in that "flow" of union with the object of your attention, you are experiencing *samadhi*.

Our yoga teacher Mary got a sweet taste of that feeling during her first *savasana*. "It was the first time I felt okay about myself in more than twenty years. I knew in my very core that I was okay, and I wanted more of that. I realized I had limited myself, been someone who was afraid to open my mouth. That experience stayed with me and led me to be more courageous." It was a dawning of realization about her life's purpose, and put her on the path to devoting her life to giving others the gift of yoga through teaching.

During one of the classes we took with her as we were writing this book, Mary shared a favorite quote from poet David Whyte: "We are the only species capable of preventing our own flowering." For Mary, the quote points to *samadhi* as a natural state that we have lost and need to find again. "An acorn has to become an oak tree. If you plant a carrot seed, it is not going to become a tomato. A cat would never try to become a horse. As humans, we cover up our light. I don't know why that is, but through the practice of yoga we can uncover it, expand it, share it, and recognize that everyone has it." Marianne Williamson describes it like this: "Love is what we are born with. Fear is what we learned here."

When we asked Mary how she would describe an "enlightened worker," she was thoughtful for a few moments. "I would say there is a palpable sense energetically. They have a smile that starts in their heart and shines through the light in their eyes. You know they are in themselves, and you want to be around them."

Csikszentmihalyi uses the term "autotelic" for what we would describe as an enlightened worker. Such people feel autonomous and independent, yet are simultaneously "fully immersed in the current of life," he says. The source of their happiness is doing the things that help them, and those around them, grow and fulfill their potential. They might be blessed with material wealth, but that is not the source of their well-being. While they may enjoy worldly pleasures, Csikszentmihalyi says, they don't *need* "entertainment, comfort, power, or fame, because so much of what they do is so rewarding."

PURPOSE, WORK, AND ABSORPTION

Soon after she was hired at a major East Coast university, Jana asked her boss to describe exactly what he wanted her to do. He answered, "I want you to take care of people." Exactly how she did that, he said, was her decision.

The university attracts graduate students from all over the country and the world. Many bring their families with them. Jana's job had been created to help these disparate educational expatriates create a community that would support the students' experience. They depended on Jana to help them and their families get oriented to a new city, figure out where to reside, and solve myriad problems of daily living. Some of them knew only a little English. Many had young children to care for without their customary support systems, and spouses who were buried in their studies. She had an official job title, but the roles she took on included advisor, teacher, cheerleader, and confidante.

By tapping into the expertise and experience of the students and their families, Jana collaborated with the community to create childcare co-ops, programs for learning and practicing English, and classes in yoga, cooking, and gardening. With Jana's help, they staged cultural awareness festivals, formed reading groups, knitting circles, art exhibits, and more.

"In crafting the tasks of the job, there was so much going on it sparked constant creativity and infectious enthusiasm," says Jana, a longtime yoga practitioner who also teaches occasionally. "I have never before worked so hard in my life—I was putting out tremendous energy. But I also received tremendous energy from the community. It was so much fun, and I had a profound sense of satisfaction."

Jana remembers this as a time of *samadhi*—being absorbed in the meaningful work of serving others. "I felt I had been planted in this fertile ground, and I blossomed. It was like . . . inhale, exhale. Where did the day go?"

Her experience mirrors one of an aspect described by Desikachar in *The Heart of Yoga*: "In *samadhi* our personal identity—name, profession, family history, bank account, and so forth—completely disappears. In a moment of *samadhi*, none of that exists anymore."

~~~~~
Five suggestions for working toward samadhi

1. Spend a few minutes reflecting about times when you felt "in the zone," completely connected and engaged in something that made you lose yourself. What were some of the key contributors to those times?

2. Understanding your purpose, then uniting that with a bigger vision, is key to experiencing *samadhi* at work. Ask yourself questions such as: "What is it I want to contribute? How can I fulfill my potential? How is what I am doing now serving that purpose?"

3. Use your answers to those questions to consider what aspects of work you could begin to look at in a way that would facilitate further developing your potential. What do you notice?

4. If you could reinvent your work life to be in better alignment with your purpose, what would it look like? What actions could you take to begin this reinvention?

5. What aspects of a yoga practice could connect you to purpose? Make a list, and develop a plan for incorporating those practices in a consistent and meaningful way.

conclusion

FINDING YOUR WAY

~~~~~~

Be gentle with yourself.
This is a long and difficult journey.

Swami Rama

~~~~~~

As I hunched over my laptop at Fair Trade Coffee, a local café and hangout near our downtown condo, from the corner of my eye I saw Howard approaching. I felt frantic about meeting the looming book deadline. What if he was in the mood for a chat? Not now. My time is valuable. I had important things to do.

Howard is a regular at the coffee house. He was usually there when I arrived, and he was still there when I left. When I worked in the café over several weeks, we had become friendly. Most of what I know of him—and it is not much—has been gleaned from overheard conversations. Like me, he takes the light rail to get to the coffee shop. Unlike me, he spends most of his day just sitting in a chair. Being.

In his eighth decade, Howard sports a shock of white hair, has piercing blue eyes and a negligible chin. He suffered a stroke a few years ago and leans heavily on a copper cane when he walks. As I watched him shuffle toward me, I didn't have to worry about making eye contact. Because of the stroke, he cannot hold his head upright. When he talks, he swivels his torso and peers up from a slightly bent position.

And then he was there, next to my table. I like Howard. I didn't want to be rude. Putting on a smile, I looked at him.

He gently put his rough hand on my shoulder. "Take a break," he said, and then immediately executed a slow pivot, returning to the ratty, black upholstered armchair that is unofficially his. I looked at the words beaming out from my computer screen and sighed. And then laughed.

Howard was right.

I got up and did a few yoga stretches.

Our original pitch to the publisher for this book was to write something that tied yoga to organizational development. We thought a book about creating work policies, rules, and regulations by using yoga principles would create stronger and more humane organizations. Our intention was to present a business case to the powerful and the influential. But our wise, wise editors suggested we write a more personal book, geared to individuals. At the conclusion of writing this, we see clearly it is a more logical, beneficial, and potentially transformational approach.

This was underscored by something our friend and colleague Margaret Wheatley said at a gathering to celebrate the twentieth anniversary of the publishing company we share, Berrett-Koehler Publishers. Meg is a prolific author whose books are filled with keen insights. She wrote a beautiful foreword for our first book, *Authentic Conversations*. As part of an authors' panel during the celebration, she asked questions that flew into our hearts: "How do I be in my work, regardless of whether it turns the world around? How do I be in my work with full conviction that it is the right work, no matter what happens?" She made it clear that she did not have answers—maybe there are no answers. We could only hold the questions together.

Meg concluded her remarks like this: "I want to be on this journey together. I want to be with other people who are similarly conscious. And I want to let go of needing to be the one who is responsible for changing the world."

And it struck me—that is one of the beautiful things about yoga. It does not command that we change the world.

It only asks us to find ourselves. It gives us the means to do so. In that discovery, the world *is* changed.

THE PROMISE OF ENDLESS EXPANSION

During our conversation with Maureen Dolan, she emphasized how encouraged she is to see yoga taking hold among workers and in many of the country's workplaces. "There are hundreds of thousands of individuals who practice yoga," Dolan says. "They bring their values and their practices to the workplace and influence their workmates. This will make a difference." She incorporated yoga into her work while teaching adults at DePaul University because she knows people are hungry for what yoga offers. Most of these adult students are workers returning to the university to get an undergraduate degree. Many come to class directly from their jobs, feeling stressed about work and family responsibilities.

"I was using a few moments at the beginning of each class to teach just a stretch or two, or a deep breathing technique, and a time of silent reflection. Many students approached me afterward and said I should design a course where people could learn yoga philosophy and go more deeply into these practices."

And so she did. More than 700 people have been through those classes, and they fill up every term. "In a particularly striking feedback loop, the system of a few moments of yoga in each class led to students inspiring me to create a course on yoga's transformative qualities." Expansion.

Laura Karet, the CEO at Giant Eagle, says the term *namasté* informs every aspect of her leadership philosophy, and she looks for ways to bake this concept into her organization. "One of the ways we do it is by emphasizing the importance of being 'title blind.' We do not accept that your title makes you superior, or smarter, or better than anyone else. Whether you are a cashier, a janitor, the CEO, or a manager, what you think and what you have to contribute to this company is equally important. That is a formal way of practicing *namasté* without using the word."

She tells a story about her father's longtime habit of chatting with tollbooth workers. He began the practice after hearing a story while studying with his rabbi about the importance of thanking those often considered "lowly" for their service. It was a practice that made her cringe as a kid, watching from the backseat as her father exchanged pleasantries with the workers while cars lined up behind them, honking.

Fast forward to a recent opening of a new grocery store. A woman approached her father and said, "Hello, Mr. Shapira." Karet watched her father's brow furrow as he asked the patron to remind him where they had met before. "You wouldn't remember me," the woman said, "but I worked in the tollbooth on the turnpike you used to drive through all the time."

But wait, Karet says. It gets better.

A few weeks later, she was driving on the turnpike and, following her father's example, said hello to the tollbooth worker and asked how she was doing. The worker said, "Do you happen to work at Giant Eagle?" Surprised, Karet replied that, yes, she did. But how did the woman in the tollbooth know? "Oh, the people who work at Giant Eagle always say hi to me," she replied.

Even though her father doesn't have a formal yoga practice, Karet says this is just one of the ways he lives out *namasté* every day. Through example, he has influenced others to do the same. Paramahansa Yogananda makes a similar observation in his book, *Autobiography of a Yogi*: "There are a number of great [people] . . . who though they may never have heard the words *yogi* or *swami*, are yet true exemplars of those terms."

YOUR LIGHT WILL MAKE A DIFFERENCE

As we did research for this book, Jamie and I were delighted to discover how many companies are incorporating yoga practices into the work day. We hope they will be inspired to expand those practices through an exploration of the richness of all eight limbs. These principles have much to contribute toward creating ethical, humane organizations and productive workplaces, where worth is measured as much by value created as by dollars earned.

And yet, it is the individual who will make the difference. *You* will make the difference. We wrote this book for you.

My friend Barclay Hudson asserts that when talk turns to the search for better "work/life balance" it is a signal that we have already given up. "We have conceded that work is a drain of energy and spirit and nourishment, and that satisfactions have to be found elsewhere, from things provided by the paycheck. We've conceded that work is a cost, a liability, a negative, while the benefits come from life on the outside." Integrating yoga practices into your life is a way to revolutionize thinking about work. It can lead to redefining "a good life as one that includes good, meaningful work as a core element, and a major purpose for living," he says.

Work is just another venue for practicing yoga. It is accessible to anyone. We echo the words of Pandit Rajmani Tigunait: "Other travelers can point the way according to their knowledge and experience, but ultimately we must walk the path."

We hope you will find this book a useful guide as you walk the path. As Meg said so eloquently, we would like to be on the journey with you. We want to travel with people who are similarly conscious.

Namasté.

GLOSSARY OF TERMS

The Eight Limbs

The *Yamas*	Universal morality	YAH-mas
ahimsa	Non-violence	a-HIM-sa
satya	Non-lying	SAT-ya
asteya	Non-stealing	ah-STAY-ya
brahmacharya	Non-squandering of vital energies	BRAH-ma-CHAR-ya
aparigraha	Non-greed, non-hoarding	Ah-PAR-ee-GRAH-ha
The *Niyamas*	Personal observances	Nee-YAH-ma
saucha	Cleanliness, purity	SOW-cha
santosha	Contentment	san-TOSH-ah
svadhyaya	Self-study	shah-VAH-adh-YA-ya
tapas	Discipline, zeal	TAH-pas
ishvara-pranidhana	Surrender	ish-VA-ra-pra-NI-dana
Asana	Physical practice, postures	AH-sana
Pranayama	Breath control	prah-na-YAH-ma
Pratyahara	Withdrawal of the senses	prat-YA-hara
Dharana	Focus, deep concentration	da-HA-rana
Dhyana	Meditation	DIE-yana
Samadhi	Absorption	sa-MAH-dhi

Other Yoga Terms

asmita	Ignorance that confuses the physical body and conscious mind with our divine self or spirit	as-MEE-ta
Bhagavad Gita	A 700–verse Hindu scripture that is part of the ancient Sanskrit epic Mahabharata. This scripture contains a conversation between prince Arjuna and his guide Krishna.	b-HAGA-vad GEE-ta
dharma	Life purpose	DAR-mah
drishti	Gazing of the eyes	DRISH-ti
mantra	A sound, syllable, word, or group of words that is considered capable of creating transformation	MAHN-tra
Patanjali	The compiler of the Yoga Sutras, an important collection of aphorisms on yoga practice	pa-TAN-jelay
prana	Life force, energy that moves through all earthly things	PRAH-na
samskara	Concept of imprints being left on the subconscious mind by experience	SAM-ska-ra
Yoga	Yoke, union, join together	
yoga *nidra*	A sleep-like state which yogis report to experience during their meditations	

RESOURCES

Introduction

Edwin F. Bryant, *The Yoga Sutras of Patanjali* (New York: North Point Press, 2009). Also recommended is *The Yoga Sutras of Patanjali*, translation and commentary by Swami Satchidananda (Buckingham, VA: Integral Yoga Publications, 2012).

Ecknath Easwaran, *Conquest of Mind* (Tomales, CA: Nilgiri Press, 2010).

Stewart Oksenhorn, "Midvalley Yogi Rod Stryker Appears at Aspen Eco Fest," *Aspen Times*, June 8, 2012.

Chapter One: Beginners Mind

Ecknath Easwaran, *Bhagavad-Gita*, translation and introduction, 2nd ed. (Tomales, CA: Blue Mountain Center of Meditation, 2007).

Rod Stryker, *The Four Desires: Creating a Life of Purpose, Happiness, Prosperity, and Freedom* (New York: Delacorte Press, 2011).

Chapter Two: The First Limb

Satya:

T. K. V. Desikachar, *The Heart of Yoga*, 2nd ed. (Rochester, VT: Inner Traditions International, 1999).

Judith and Ike Lasater, *What We Say Matters: Practicing Non-Violent Communication* (Berkeley, CA: Rodmell Press, 2009).

Brahmacharya:

Jaganath Carrera, *Inside the Yoga Sutras: A Comprehensive Source* (Buckingham, VT: Integral Yoga Publishers, 2006).

Charles Duhigg, *The Power of Habit: Why We Do What We Do in Life and Business* (New York: Random House, 2012).

Aparigraha:

Marzenna Jakubczak, "Towards Knowing Ourselves: Classical Yoga Perspective," *Journal of Human Values* 10 (October 2004): 111–116.

Chapter Three: The Second Limb

Svadhyaya:

Bill George, *True North Groups: A Powerful Path to Personal and Leadership Development* (San Francisco: Berrett-Koehler, 2011).

Peter Bregman, *18 Minutes: Find Your Focus, Master Distraction and Get the Right Things Done* (New York: Business Plus, 2012).

Larry Dressler, *Standing in the Fire: Leading High-Heat Meetings with Clarity, Calm and Courage* (San Francisco: Berrett-Koehler, 2010).

Tapas:

Pema Chodron, *When Things Fall Apart: Heart Advice for Difficult Times* (Boston: Shambhala Library, 2002).

Kevin Cashman, *Leadership from the Inside Out: Becoming a Leader for Life* (San Franscisco: Berrett-Koehler, 2008).

Chapter Four: The Third Limb

P. Tekur, C. Singphow, H. R. Nagendra, and N. Raghuram, "Effect of Short-Term Intensive Yoga Program on Pain, Functional Disability, and Spinal Flexibility in Chronic Low Back Pain," *Journal of Alternative and Complementary Medicine* (July 2008): 637–644.

Chapter Six: The Fifth Limb

David Frawley, "Pratyahara: The Forgotten Limb of Yoga," available at www.abuddhistlibrary.com.

Pico Iyer, *The Open Road: The Global Journey of the Fourteenth Dali Lama* (New York: Knopf, 2008).

Chapter Seven: The Sixth Limb

Walter Isaacson, *Steve Jobs* (New York: Simon & Schuster, 2011).

Michael Singer, *The Untethered Soul: The Journey Beyond Yourself* (Oakland, CA: New Harbinger Publications and Noetic Books, 2007).

Chapter Eight: The Seventh Limb

Joe Dispenza, *Breaking the Habit of Being Yourself: How to Lose Your Mind and Create a New One* (New York: Hays House, 2012).

S. B. Khalsa, S. M. Shorter, S. Cope, G. Wyshak, and E. Sklar, "Yoga Ameliorates Performance Anxiety and Mood Disturbance in Young Professional Musicians," *Applied Psychophysiology and Biofeedback* (December 2009): 279–289.

S. W. Lazar, G. Bush, R. L. Gollub, G. L. Fricchione, G. Khalsa, and H. Benson, "Functional Brain Mapping of the Relaxation Response and Meditation," *NeuroReport* 11 (2000): 1581–1585.

Y. Y. Tang and M. I. Posner, "Attention Training and Attention State Training," *Trends in Cognitive Sciences* 5 (2009): 222–227.

Chapter Nine: The Eighth Limb

T. K. V. Desikachar, *The Heart of Yoga*, 2nd ed. (Rochester, VT: Inner Traditions International, 1999).

Conclusion

Barclay Hudson, "Have a Cup of Tea," unpublished paper, 2012.

Margaret Wheatley, *So Far From Home: Lost and Found in Our Brave New World* (San Francisco: Berrett-Koehler, 2012).

Paramahansa Yogananda, *Autobiography of a Yogi*, 13th edition (Los Angeles: Self-Realization Fellowship Publishing, 1998).

Resources

Joseph Goldstein, *The Experience of Insight: A Simple and Direct Guide to Buddhist Meditation* (Boston: Shambala Publications, 1976).

Thich Naht Hanh, *The Miracle of Mindfulness: An Introduction to the Art of Meditation* (Boston: Beacon Press, 1999).

Jack Kornfield, *Meditation for Beginners* (Louisville, CO: True Sounds, 2008).

Rolf Sovik, *Moving Inward: The Journey to Meditation* (Honesdale, PA: Himalayan Institute, 2005).

ACKNOWLEDGMENTS

If this page of acknowledgements was as full as our grateful hearts, it would be never ending. Countless people have served the roles of doula and midwife to this book—some are named here, but many more are not. Please know we hold you all close in our hearts.

We are deeply indebted, as are our readers, to every one of you who breathed life into these concepts by sharing your stories with us and living lives that are shining examples of the power of yoga.

We feel deep gratitude for all the teachers who have influenced Jamie and me—but most especially to Mary Bruce, Jenn Chiarelli, Ron and Nancy Dubinsky, Mary Beth Markus, Lynn Matthews, Kat Myers, and Mark Roberts. Another shout of gratitude goes out to my Master Immersion sangha. The energy with which they surrounded me when this book began to germinate was inspirational: Amy Andrews, Nan Aton, LaBarbara Daliwahl, Danielle Gardner, Kathie Holligan, Susan Jarvie, Ed Laniado, Linda Santopietro, Karen Santini, Kari Schmul, Carrie Sweeney, Erica Vucich, and Mary Wimmer.

We so appreciate the help and support of so many friends—Kathryn Adams, Marjorie Adler, Katherine Armstrong, Noah Blumenthal, Donna Jo Carney, Kevin Cashman, Tim Cothron, Joann Dornich, Howard Fox, Barclay Hudson, Jennifer Kahnweiler, Barbara McAfee, Jeanine Mumford, Angela Rogers, Margie Weaver, and Leslie Yerkes. Thank you, Sparks, for cheering us on: Reg Blakely,

Jennifer Barnes, Sharon and Peter Flanagan-Hyde, Robin Postel, Reuben Sanchez, and Christine Whitney-Sanchez.

Nancy McVicar Drake, wherever you are, thank you for persuading me to join the yoga group at the *Sun-Sentinel*.

Daphne Atkeson is not only is a dear and longtime friend, she has been a superlative accountability partner, cheerleader, and writing coach all wrapped up into one beautiful package. I cannot thank her enough. We're also grateful to those who read our first draft and gave us invaluable feedback: Danielle Goodman, Elianne Obadia, Dan Siegel, Lauren Walker, and Ulf Wolf.

Tricia McCarty and Mike Morchak, we will always bless your light-filled hearts.

We are so blessed to belong to the most marvelous BK author tribe, whose members are a constant source of inspiration and support. I am particularly thankful to those who show up in the cold, dark morning hours during author retreats and allow me the gift of teaching yoga. We will forever feel beholden to the blue-chip Berrett-Koehler crew, *all of them* are rock stars! But we want to give special thanks to our editors, Neal Maillet, Steve Piersanti, and Jeevan Sivasubramaniam.

And finally, we cannot overstate our gratitude to our loving and supportive families. We both were blessed with exemplary parents: Jean and James Showkeir and Arlene and Maurice Bateman. Our children, Sonnet, Skyler, Zackery, and JR, and our grandson, Kadin, are the lights of our lives.

INDEX

absorption/union/enlightenment
(*samadhi*), x, 172–81, 191
meaning of, 14–15, 173–74, 180,
191
and purpose of one's work and
life, 177–80, 181
suggestions for practice, 181
vignettes on, 172–73, 175–76
abundance, 67–69, 71. *See also*
non-greed (*aparigraha*)
accountability, 116–17
adho mukha (handstand), 94–95
ahimsa (non-violence), x, 22, 23–33,
74, 191
anger, 27, 29, 88–92, 103–5, 107,
135, 164
aparigraha (non-greed), x, 22, 63–71,
74
Apple, 124, 153, 164–65
ardha chandrasana (half-moon pose),
128
Aristotle, 94
asana (postures), x, 12, 14, 16–17, 35,
55, 77, 83, 94–95, 112, 115,
121–29, 191
asmita (confusion of body/mind with
divine self), 66, 192
asteya (non-stealing), x, 22, 47–54,
74, 191
Atman (deeper Self), 9
attachment, 26, 43, 61, 68-70, 88-89,
114-16, 119, 127. *See also*
detachment
Authentic Conversations (Showkeir
and Showkeir), 4–5, 36, 41,
159, 185
authenticity, 103, 107–8
Autobiography of a Yogi (Yogananda),
188
ayama (control), 132

balance, 13, 126, 128, 188–89. *See
also* non-squandering of vital
energies (*brahmacharya*)
Bartz, Carol, 40
Bateson, Mary Catherine, 73
Be the Hero (Blumenthal), 166–67
beginner's mind, 8
Benson, Herbert, 163
Bhagavad Gita, 13, 15, 89, 115–16,
192
Bharati, Swami Jnaneshvara, 61
Bikram yoga, 23–24, 35–36

blame, 30–31, 37, 115
Blue Mountain Center of Meditation,
9
Blumenthal, Noah, 166–67
body. *See* postures (*asana*); purity
(*saucha*)
brahmacharya (non-squandering of
vital energies), x, 22, 55–62,
74, 191
Breaking the Habit of Being Yourself
(Dispenza), 163
breath control (*pranayama*), 131–40
alternate nostril breathing (*nadi
shodhana*), 135, 138, 139–40
asana (postures) and, 14
for children, 134–35
cleansing lungs through, 77
cooling breath (*sitali*), 140
definition of, 17, 191
difficulty of, 133–34
grounding and emotional control
through, 136–37
lion's breath (*simhasana*), 139
and pace of conversation, 132,
133–34, 137–38
and redirecting energy, 134–36
research on physical and mental
benefits of, 136–37
self-study (*svadhyaya*) and, 103–4
suggestions for practice, 137–38
"take five" breathing technique
for focus, 160
techniques of, 139–40
vignettes on, 132–36
visualization during, 134–35, 137
Bregman, Peter, 105–6
Bruce, Mary, 3, 4, 5, 147–48
Buddha, 35

Caasdan, Robin, 112
Carrera, Jaganath, 57
Cashman, Kevin, 98
celibacy, 56, 57, 59
chattaranga (push-up), 94
children, 96–97, 105, 106, 134–35,
146, 180
Chinmoy, Sri, 161
Chodron, Pema, 10, 95
Choudhury, Bikram, 21
cleanliness. *See* purity (*saucha*)
compassion, 26, 31–32, 74, 79, 86,
91–92, 115, 163–64

conduct code. *See* personal conduct (*niyamas*)
Conquest of the Mind (Easwaran), 9, 67, 164
contentment (*santosha*), 83–93
  attachment versus, 88–89
  as choice, 85–88
  and control of outcome, 89–90
  and dedication to excellence at work, 89–90
  and desire without attachment, 88–89
  and detachment from one's stories, 90–92, 93
  gratitude and, 87–90, 93
  judgment getting in way of, 86, 91–92
  non-greed (*aparigraha*) and, 84
  as precept of Second Limb of yoga, x, 75, 191
  suggestions for practice, 92–93
  vignettes on, 83, 85–87, 90
cravings, control of, 60–62, 78
Csikszentmihalyi, Mihaly, 174, 179

Day, Christine, vii–viii
De Rham, Cat, 75
decluttering, 81, 82
Desikachar, T. K. V., 41–42, 95, 142, 175, 180
desire, 88–89, 100, 159
detachment. *See also* attachment; surrender (*ishvara-pranidhana*)
  Bhagavad Gita on, 116
  from desire, 159
  mantra for, 119
  non-greed and, 68–70
  from one's stories, 90–92, 93
  from outcomes, 114–16, 119, 127
Devi, Nischala Joy, 57
dharana (focus), x, 14, 17, 152–60, 175, 191
dharma (life's purpose), 178, 192
dhyana (meditation), x, 14, 17–18, 96, 162–69, 175, 191
diet and nutrition, 77–78, 81
discipline (*tapas*), 94–100
  asana practice and, 77
  for children, 96–97, 134–35
  desire and, 100
  energy draining versus energy restoring activities, 100
  excellence and, 96, 127
  meditation and, 96
  motivation and, 99, 100
  and regeneration to restore energy, 97–100, 127

rest and, 97–98, 127
suggestions for practice, 100
time management and, 97–99
translation of *tapas* as heat, 95
vignettes on, 94–95, 96–97
Dispenza, Joe, 163
divine/divinity, 9, 18, 66, 92, 192. *See also* absorption/union/enlightenment (*samadhi*); surrender (*ishvara-pranidhana*)
Dolan, Maureen, 59–60, 96, 113–14, 186
Dressler, Larry, 108
drishti (gaze), 154, 192
Duhigg, Charles, 60–61
Dunn, Elizabeth, 66–67

Easwaran, Eknath, 9, 15, 67, 96, 163–64
Eat, Pray, Love (Gilbert), 174
eating habits, 77–78, 81
Edison, Thomas, 23
ego satisfaction, 23–24, 66–67, 88–89. *See also* attachment
Eight Limbs of Yoga, x, 6–8, 12–18, 173, 178, 191. *See also* yoga; *and specific limbs*
18 Minutes (Bregman), 105
Eighth Limb of yoga. *See* absorption/ union/enlightenment (*samadhi*)
emotional intelligence, 102–3, 165
energy. *See* breath control (*pranayama*); discipline (*tapas*)
enlightenment. *See* absorption/ union/enlightenment (*samadhi*)
ethics in workplace, 29–30
excellence, 89–90, 94, 96, 127

Farhi, Donna, 51
Faulds, Donna, 151
fear
  breath control (*pranayama*) and, 133–34
  of change, 118
  contentment (*santosha*) in face of, 85–86, 90
  detachment from, 116
  as learned response, 179
  non-lying (*satya*) in face of, 38, 39, 43
  non-violence (*ahimsa*) in face of, 25, 28, 29, 33
  and surrendering to resistance, 117
feedback on performance, 42, 106–7, 111
Fifth Limb of yoga. *See* sense withdrawal (*pratyahara*)
First Limb of yoga. See moral code (*yamas*)

focus (*dharana*), x, 14, 17, 152–60, 191
    absorption (*samadhi*) and, 175
    accidental *dharana*, 154–55
    during balancing poses, 154–55
    listening and, 158–59, 160
    meditation and, 153–54
    and multitasking as myth,
        155–57
    and present moment as gift, 159
    suggestions for practice, 160
    "take five" breathing technique
        for, 160
    vignettes on, 152, 157–58
    work boundaries for, 157–58
food. *See* diet and nutrition
"For My Wedding" (Henley), 64, 70
forearm balance (*pincha myurasana*),
    94
Four Desires, The (Stryker), 89
Fourth Limb of yoga. *See* breath
    control (*pranayama*)
Frankl, Viktor, 88
Frawley, David, 142, 143

Gandhi, Indira, 121
Gandhi, Mahatma, 25, 57, 88
Gates, Rolf, 168
General Mills, 124, 164–65
generosity, 49, 53–54, 66–67, 71. *See
    also* non-stealing (*asteya*)
George, William, 103
Giant Eagle, 103–4, 128, 186–88
Gilbert, Elizabeth, 174
Gill, Michèle, 75
Google, 124, 165
gratitude, 64, 69–70, 71, 87–90, 93,
    101, 107. *See also* content-
    ment (*santosha*)
greed, 64–66. *See also* non-greed
    (*aparigraha*)

habits
    change of, 60–61, 95, 102, 105–6
    definition of *samskara*, 192
    eating habits, 77–78, 81
    excellence as, 94
    of organized work environment,
        81, 82
    power of, 60–61
    self-study and, 102
    of swearing, 79–82
half-moon pose (*ardha chandrasana*),
    128
handstand (*adho mukha*), 94–95
happiness, 66–67, 88
headstand (*salamba sirusana*), 94
health, 77–78

Heart of Yoga, The (Desikachar),
    41–42, 142, 180
helplessness, 85–86, 115
Henley, Don, 64, 70
Henning, Joel, 52, 88
Himalayan Institute, 25, 84–85
hoarding. *See* greed; non-greed
    (*aparigraha*)
honesty. *See* non-lying (*satya*)
Hudson, Barclay, 13, 102, 177,
    188–89
humility, 49–51, 101, 128

IGE. *See* Institute for Global Ethics
    (IGE)
Inside the Yoga Sutras (Carrera), 57
Institute for Global Ethics (IGE), 39
intention. *See also* focus (*dharana*);
    moral code (*yamas*); personal
    conduct (*niyamas*)
    asana practice as metaphor for,
        126
    and detachment from outcome,
        114
    and Eight Limbs of Yoga, 14–15
    of expansion, 112–13
    for meditation, 169
    for non-violence (*ahimsa*)
        practice, 34
    self-study and, 102, 107
    sharing and feedback on, 54
introspection. *See* self-study
    (*svadhyaya*)
Isaacson, Walter, 153–54
ishvara-pranidhana (surrender), x, 75,
    112–19, 191
Iyengar, BKS, 47
Iyer, Pico, 143

Jakubczak, Marzenna, 66
Jobs, Steve, 153–54
Johnson, Robert, 22
Jois, Sri K. Pattabhi, 6
judgment, 44–45, 86, 91–92
Jung, Carl, 12

Karet, Laura, 103–4, 128, 186–88
karma, 15
Katha Upanishad, 55
Kenison, Katrina, 168
Khalsa, Sat Bir, 164
King, Martin Luther, Jr., 88
Kripalu, Swami, 95
Krishamurti, Jiddu, 101
Kriya Yoga, 59
Kriyananda, Swami, 160
Kundalini Yoga, 95

Lasater, Judith Hanson and Ike K., 44
Lazar, Sara, 164
leadership and management
    attachment and, 89
    "bonus equality" and, 52
    demands on, 91, 98
    leadership philosophy of, 128,
        186–87
    micromanaging, 51
    non-lying (*satya*) and, 38–39
    non-stealing (*asteya*) and, 51–52
    non-violence (*ahimsa*) and, 28–29
    and "open door" work culture,
        157–58
    productive relationship with
        manager, 42
    self-acceptance and, 128
    self-study (*svadhyaya*) and, 104
    stealing credit and, 52
    "thought leader," 5
    work feedback and, 42, 106–7
Leadership from the Inside Out
    (Cashman), 98
lion's breath (*simhasana*), 139
listening, 36, 42–46, 158–59.
Lord of the Dance pose (*natarajasana*),
    152
lying. *See* non-lying (*satya*)

management. *See* leadership and
    management
Mandela, Nelson, 88
manipulation, 39–41
Man's Search for Meaning (Frankl), 88
mantras, 119, 169, 192
Markus, Mary Beth and Vince, 86–87
Matthews, Mary, 5
McCall, Timothy, 61
medical care, 108–10, 132, 144–46,
    148–49, 162–63, 175–77
meditation (*dhyana*), 162–69
    absorption (*samadhi*) and, 175
    Blumenthal's technique for, 167
    for children, 97, 134–35
    discipline (*tapas*) and, 96
    in Eight Limbs of Yoga, x, 191
    focus (*dharana*) and, 153–54
    mantra for, 169
    purposes of, 163
    research on benefits of, 163–64
    solo practice of, 166–68, 169
    suggestions for practice, 169
    theme or intention for, 169
    Transcendental Meditation, 165
    vignettes on, 162–63, 165–66
    workplace benefits of, 17–18,
        164–66, 169
    yoga *nidra*, 4–5, 192

Meditations from the Mat (Gates and
    Kenison), 168
mind-body awareness, 78–80
mindfulness. *See also* presence and
    present moment
    of breath, 17, 133, 134–40
    and Eight Limbs of Yoga
        generally, 16
    instinctual mindfulness and,
        147–49
    of labeling and judging others,
        44–45
    meditation (*dhyana*) and, 17–18,
        163–64
    research on mindfulness
        meditation, 163–64
    self-study (*svadhyaya*) and, 105
    of taking things not freely given,
        49, 53
    of vocabulary choices, 79
"monkey mind," 2
moral code (*yamas*)
    non-greed (*aparigraha*), 63–71
    non-lying (*satya*), 35–46
    non-squandering of vital energies
        (*brahmacharya*), 55–62
    non-stealing (*asteya*), x, 22, 47–54
    non-violence (*ahimsa*), x, 22,
        23–33
    overview of, x, 14–16, 191
    Patanjali on, 22
    precepts of, 15–16, 22, 191
    relationship between *niyamas*
        (personal conduct) and, 16
    suggestions for practice, 33–34,
        45–46, 62, 71
    symbiotic relationship within,
        41–42, 60, 74
motivation, 65–66, 99, 100
multitasking, 155–57

nadi shodhana (alternate nostril
    breathing), 135, 138, 139–40
namasté, 9–10, 186–87
natarajasana (Lord of the Dance
    pose), 152
Nhat Hahn, Thich, 21, 133
niyamas. *See* personal conduct
    (*niyamas*)
non-attachment. *See* contentment
    (*santosha*); detachment
non-greed (*aparigraha*), x, 63–71, 191
    abundance perspective and,
        67–69, 71
    accountability and, 117
    "bonus equality" and, 52
    confusing pleasure and profits
        with purpose, 66–67

non-greed (*continued*)
  contentment (*santosha*) and, 84
  generosity and, 66–67, 71
  gratitude and, 64, 69–70, 71, 88
  implications of, at work, 67–69
  interrelationships among First
      Limb precepts, 74
  and letting go of yearning, 69–70
  and needs versus wants, 71
  and reasons for working, 65–66,
      70, 71, 74
  and staying in the moment, 70
  suggestions for practice, 71
  vignettes on, 63–64, 68–70
  and work motivated by love and
      service, 65–66
  at yoga studio, 74
non-lying (*satya*), x, 22, 35–46, 191
  and CEOs and senior managers,
      38–39
  as core value, 39
  elements of truth, 36–38
  and interrelationships among
      First Limb precepts, 41–42,
      60, 74
  kindness and, 36, 41–43
  and listening to others' perspec-
      tives, 36, 42–46
  manipulation and "spin" versus,
      39–41
  "right speech" and, 36, 46
  risk in, at work, 37–38
  self-study (*svadhyaya*) and, 110
  silence as violation of, 43–45, 110
  suggestions for practice, 45–46
  trust and, 37, 38–39
  vignettes on, 35–36, 42
  at yoga studio, 74
non-squandering of vital energies
      (*brahmacharya*), x, 22, 55–62,
      191
  and control of sensual cravings,
      60–62, 78
  and interrelationships among
      First Limb precepts, 60, 74
  and power of habits, 60–61
  sexual energy and, 56–60, 62
  suggestions for practice, 62
  vignettes on, 55, 58–59
non-stealing (*asteya*), x, 22, 47–54, 191
  "bonus equality" and, 52
  examples of stealing at work, 48–52
  generosity and, 49, 53–54
  and humility and self-restraint,
      49–51
  and interrelationships among
      First Limb precepts, 60, 74

micromanaging versus, 51
self-reliance and, 51
stealing credit and, 52
suggestions for practice, 54
tardiness as stealing, 47–48
time theft and, 50–51, 54
vignettes on, 47–48, 50–51, 53–54
at yoga studio, 74
non-violence (*ahimsa*), x, 22, 23–33,
      191
  blame and, 30–31
  to colleagues at work, 27–29
  compassion and, 31–32, 74, 79
  diet and, 77–78
  and interrelationships among
      First Limb precepts, 41–42,
      74
  and non-squandering of vital
      energies (*brahmacharya*), 60
  to self, 23–27
  self-to-self conversations, 25–26,
      33
  speaking up about dangerous or
      unethical conditions,
      29–30
  suggestions for practice, 33–34
  for supervisors, managers, and
      leaders, 28–29
  swearing as violation of, 79–82
  vignettes on, 23–24, 26
  in violent situations, 28–29,
      32–33
  and vocabulary choices, 79–80
  work habits and, 24–25, 33
  at yoga studio, 74
Norton, Michael, 66–67
nutrition. *See* diet and nutrition

Oliver, Mary, 131
Open Road, The (Iyer), 143
Oz, Mehmet, 165

paschimottanasana (seated forward
      bend), 83
Patanjali, 6, 8, 22, 66, 88–89, 155,
      192. *See also* Sutras
peace. *See* sense withdrawal
      (*pratyahara*)
perfectionism, 83, 127
personal conduct (*niyamas*)
  contentment (*santosha*), x, 75,
      83–93
  discipline (*tapas*), x, 75, 94–100
  overview of, x, 14–16, 191
  purity (*saucha*), x, 75, 76–82
  relationship between *yamas*
      (moral code) and, 16

self-study (*svadhyaya*), x, 75, 101–11
    suggestions for practice, 81–82,
        92–93, 100, 110–11, 118–19
    surrender (*ishvara-pranidhana*), x,
        75, 112–19
    symbiotic relationship within, 74
physical practice. *See* postures (*asana*)
pincha myurasana (forearm balance),
    94
Posner, Michael, 164
postures (*asana*), x, 14, 121–29, 191
    alignment and, 123–24
    breath control and, 14, 77
    corporate sponsorship of yoga
        classes, 124–25, 129
    focus during balancing poses, 154–55
    forearm balance (*pincha
        myurasana*), 94
    half-moon pose (*ardha chan-
        drasana*), 128
    handstand (*adho mukha*), 94–95
    headstand (*salamba sirusana*), 94
    Lord of the Dance pose (*natara-
        jasana*), 152
    and metaphors for qualities
        needed for work success,
        126–28
    as one part of spectrum of yoga,
        12
    physical and mental benefits of,
        16–17, 77, 123–26, 128
    push-up (*chattaranga*), 94
    reclining hero pose (*supta
        virasana*), 35
    resistance to, 94–95, 117
    resting pose (*savasana*), 2, 14, 55,
        122, 178
    seated forward bend (*paschimotta-
        nasana*), 83
    suggestions for pracice, 128–29
    sun salutation, 128
    vignettes on, 94–95, 122–26
    Warrior II pose, 112, 115
potential
    contentment (*santosha*) and, 84
    non-squandering of vital energies
        (*brahmacharya*) and, 60
    non-stealing (*asteya*) and, 49
    non-violence (*ahimsa*) and, 25
    obstacles to development of, 75
    postures (*asana*) and, 127–28
    self-discipline (*tapas*) and, 95
    self-study (*svadhyaya*) and, 102, 105
    work as metaphor for, 18
    yoga for development of, 3, 6–11,
        14–15

Power of Habit (Duhigg), 60–61
prana (energy of life force), 132, 192
pranayama (breath control), x, 14, 17,
    77, 96, 131–40, 191
pratyahara (sense withdrawal), x, 14,
    17, 141–50, 175, 191
presence and present moment, 70,
    95, 108, 158, 159. *See also*
    mindfulness
purity (*saucha*), x, 75, 76–82, 191
    bodily cleanliness and, 77–78
    diet and, 77–78, 81
    health and well-being, 77–78
    mind-body awareness and, 78–80
    for organized work environment,
        81, 82
    suggestions for practice, 81–82
    swearing as violation of, 79–82
    vignettes on, 76, 78–80
push-up (*chattaranga*), 94

Rama, Swami, 25, 141, 183
reclining hero pose (*supta virasana*),
    35
reflection. *See* self-study (*svadhyaya*)
resistance, surrendering to, 116–18
rest, 97–98, 127
resting pose (*savasana*), 2, 14, 55,
    122, 178
road rage, 80
Roberts, Mark, 122–23
Ryan, Michelle, 74

safety in workplace, 28–30
Sagan, Carl, 106
salamba sirusana (headstand), 94
samadhi (union, absorption,
    enlightenment), x, 14–15, 18,
    172–81, 191
samskaras (habits), 60–61, 79, 192.
    See also habits
santosha (contentment), x, 75, 83–93,
    191
Satchidananda, Swami, 57, 88–89
satya (non-lying), x, 22, 35–46, 74, 191
saucha (cleanliness, purity), x, 75,
    76–82, 191
savasana (resting pose), 2, 14, 55,
    122, 178
scarcity perspective, 68–69
Search Inside Yourself (Tan), 165
seated forward bend (*paschimottana-
    sana*), 83
Second Limb of yoga. *See* personal
    conduct (*niyamas*)
self-awareness. *See* self-study
    (*svadhyaya*)
self-confidence, 108

self-discipline. *See* discipline (*tapas*)
self-realization. *See* absorption/
    union/enlightenment
    (*samadhi*)
self-restraint, 49–51. *See also*
    discipline (*tapas*)
self-study (*svadhyaya*), x, 75, 101–11,
    191
    authenticity and, 103, 107–8
    benefits of, 102–3
    breath control and, 103–4
    core values and, 111
    cultivation of, 102
    and doing versus being, 102
    feedback and, 106–7, 111
    internal focus and outward gaze
        in, 103–6
    labels associated with the self, 111
    mindfulness and, 105
    questions for, 107
    and seeds of certainty, 106–10
    self-confidence and, 108
    sources of inspiration and, 104–5
    suggestions for practice, 110–11
    vignettes on, 101, 103–10
self-talk, 25–26, 33, 95
sense withdrawal (*pratyahara*), x, 14,
    17, 141–50, 191
    absorption (*samadhi*) and, 175
    as antidote to sensory overload,
        142–44, 146, 149
    at bedtime, 150
    freedom through, 144
    instinctual mindfulness and,
        147–49
    meaning of, 142, 191
    and mental mastery of external
        senses, 146–47
    silent retreat and, 149–50
    suggestions for practice, 149–50
    technology fast and, 149
    vignettes on, 142, 144–49
Seventh Limb of yoga. *See* medita-
    tion (*dhyana*)
sexual energy, 56–60, 62
sexual harassment/assault, 56, 59–60
Shapira, David, 103–4, 187–88
Shivananda, Swami, 146
Showkeir, Jamie
    Bikram yoga and, 35–36
    bio of, 207–8
    breath control (*pranayama*) and,
        133–34
    Henning as former business
        partner of, 52, 88
    marriage of, 59, 64

meditation and *asana* practices
    of, 8, 35–36
New York Times interview of, 133–34
as organizational consultant, 4,
    52, 88, 91
work principles and philosophies
    of, 4, 6–7
and writing *Authentic Conversa-
    tion*, 4–5
yoga analogy of, 12
Showkeir, Maren
    asana practice of, 94–95
    Bikram yoga and, 23–24, 35
    bio of, 206–7
    early yoga experiences of, 2–3,
        12–13
    marriage of, 59, 64
    as newspaper journalist, 4, 12,
        42–43, 52, 68, 122, 157–58
    work principles and philosophies
        of, 6–7
    and writing *Authentic Conversa-
        tion*, 4–5
    yoga teacher training for, 3, 4, 8,
        9, 36, 123
Shraddhananda, Swami, 59
silence, 36, 43–45, 149–50 . *See also*
    sense withdrawal (*pratyahara*)
simhasana (lion's breath), 139
Singer, Michael, 153
sitali (cooling breath), 140
Sivananda, Swami, 56, 83
Sixth Limb of yoga. *See* focus (*dharana*)
Spirit of Yoga, The (de Rham and Gill),
    75
squandering of vital energies. *See*
    non-squandering of vital
    energies (*brahmacharya*)
Srinivasan, M. S., 65–66
Standing in the Fire (Dressler), 108
stealing, 47–52. *See also* non-stealing
    (*asteya*)
stories, detachment from, 90–92, 93
stress reduction, 123, 125, 126, 134,
    135, 137, 164
Stryker, Rod, 7, 11, 89, 152
sun salutation, 128
supta virasana (reclining hero pose),
    35
surrender (*ishvara-pranidhana*), x, 75,
    112–19, 191
    accountability and, 116–17
    and awareness of one's attach-
        ments, 119
    and detachment from outcomes,
        114–16, 119, 127
    difficulty of, 113

fear of change and, 118
freedom and, 114, 115
implications of, at work, 116–19
interconnectedness and, 114
mantra for, 119
meaning of, 113–14, 118, 191
refusal to, 118–19
to resistance, 116–18
suggestions for practice, 118–19
vignettes on, 112–15
Sutras
on *asmita* (confusion of body/
mind with divine self), 66
on desire, 88–89
focus of, 6, 15, 22
on non-squandering of vital
energies (*brahmacharya*), 57
Patanjali as author of, 6, 8
on *samadhi*, 173, 174
on sense withdrawal (*pratyahara*),
144
on studying, 104
Suu Kyi, Aung San, 88
svadhyaya (self-study), x, 75, 101–11,
191
swearing, 79–82

Tan, Chade-Meng, 165
Tang, Yi-Yuan, 164
Tao Te Ching, 1
tapas (discipline, energy, zeal), x, 75,
94–100, 191
Thich Nhat Hahn, 21, 133
THINK (True, Helpful, Impoves upon
the silence, Necessary, Kind),
36
Third Limb of yoga. *See* postures
(*asana*)
Tigunait, Pandit Rajmani, 25, 84–85,
174, 189
time and time management, 50–51,
54, 97–99, 174
Transcendental Meditation (TM), 165
True North (George), 103
trust, 37, 38–39, 163
truth-telling. *See* non-lying (*satya*)

Ueshiba, Morihei, 76
union. *See* absorption/union/
enlightenment (*samadhi*)
Untethered Soul (Singer), 153

violence, 28–29, 32–33, 105, 135–36.
See also non-violence (*ahimsa*)
Vishnu mudra, 139
Vivekananda, Swami, 7

Warrior II pose, 112, 115
wealth, 66–69. *See also* greed
What We Say Matters (Lasater and
Lasater), 44
Wheatley, Margaret, 185, 189
When Things Fall Apart (Chodron), 95
Whyte, David, 178
Wilde, Oscar, 43
Wilson, Glenn, 156
Winfrey, Oprah, 165
withdrawing sensation. *See* sense
withdrawal (*pratyahara*)
work. *See* leadership and management; yoga; *and specific limbs
of yoga*
work habits, 24–25, 33
work-life balance, 13, 188–89

yamas. *See* moral code (*yamas*)
yoga. *See also* Bikram yoga; Eight
Limbs of Yoga; Sutras; *and
specific limbs and precepts of
yoga*
benefits of, at work, 6–8, 13–14,
16–18, 124–26
Bhagavad Gita on meaning of, 89
for children, 96–97, 134–35
corporate sponsorship of yoga
classes, 124–25, 129
glossary, pronunciation guide for,
191–92
influence of, on personal lifestyle
and work, 2–5, 184–89
as lifelong practice, 19
philosophical underpinnings of,
12–14
physical and mental benefits of,
2, 8, 9–10, 12, 16–17, 77,
123–26
popularity of, 7
Sanskrit meaning of word, 9
teacher training for, 3, 4, 8, 9, 36,
123
yoga *nidra*, 4–5, 192
Yogananda, Paramahansa, 188
Yogi, Maharishi Mahesh, 7, 174

zeal. *See tapas* (discipline, energy, zeal)
Zenji, Dogen, 171

ABOUT THE AUTHORS

 **Maren Showkeir** is a writer, ediitor, teacher, and yogini whose work is dedicated to helping individuals and organizations unleash their full potentials. Her passion for writing led her to a career in newspaper journalism. She had extraordinary experiences for nearly 25 years and managed to exit the industry in the nick of time. As a Knight Fellow for the International Center for Journalists in 2003–2004, she taught at universities in Buenos Aires, Argentina, and Lima, Peru, as part of a mission to promote "quality journalism worldwide in the belief that independent, vigorous media are crucial to improving the human condition." She also collaborated with local journalists to provide educational workshops for reporters and editors in the provinces who had scant opportunities for formal training.

Returning to the United States in 2005, she began a search for different meaningful work that would feed her soul. She found it through two seminal occurrences that happened at nearly the same time: she met Jamie Showkeir, an organizational consultant, and enrolled in a yoga teacher-training class with Mary Bruce at the Southwest Institute of Healing Arts. Joining *henning-showkeir & associates, inc.* as a managing partner, she discovered a satisfying new career, true love, a business partner, and a husband. Her yoga studies gave her a spiritual practice that kept her connected to something larger than herself. Those two paths have converged in the writing of this book.

Maren is the co-author (with Jamie) of *Authentic Conversations: Moving from Manipulation to Truth and Commitment* (Berrett-Koehler, 2008). She earned a BA degree in journalism from Arizona State University and an MA in Human and Organization Development at Fielding Graduate University.

Some of her very best work is reflected in the shining lives of two loving, responsible human beings, her children, Sonnet Bingham Aguirre and Skyler Bingham. She also is stepmother to Zak and JR Showkeir, and Nana Maren to grandson Kadin Chaira. Together, she and Jamie are raising Bodhi the cat. They live happily together in downtown Phoenix, Arizona.

Jamie Showkeir By family tradition and personal passion, learning has always been a calling for Jamie. It has played a pivotal role in his life and profession from his early career as an industrial arts teacher and high school football coach to his current work with those seeking to transform themselves and their organizations.

Whether working with educators, executives, business consultants, or young people just beginning their careers, his aim is to stimulate thinking, encouraging people to confront their own contributions to difficult issues and to be accountable to themselves and for the common good. At its core, Jamie's philosophy is that we are each responsible for our own choices, accountability, and motivation. As a consultant committed to collaboration and partnership, he engages his clients in creating powerful personal learning experiences.

Jamie is co-founder and owner of *henning-showkeir & associates, inc.*, a consulting business whose client list is extensive and varied. He is co-author (with Maren) of *Authentic Conversations: Moving from Manipulation to Truth and Commitment* (Berrett-Kohler, 2008). This book is based on the premise that all change is conversational first, and engaging others authentically leads to relationships and organizations we can believe in.

Jamie received a BS from Miami University in industrial/business education, where he was also a scholarship athlete. He received his MA from Eastern Michigan University in Educational Leadership. He began a meditation practice in 1972 and has practiced yoga since 2005. He served as president of the Autism Society of Michigan and is currently on the board of directors of Berrett-Koehler Publishers, Inc. Cycling, music, reading, and college football are among the ways he spends leisure time.

Jamie is father to Zak and JR Showkeir and stepfather to Sonnet Bingham Aguirre, Skyler Bingham, and Jeanine Mumford. His grandson, Kadin Chaira, and Bodhi the cat bring great joy to his life.

HENNING–SHOWKEIR & ASSOCIATES, INC.

Helping to create organizations that harmonize the demand for business results with the individual's need to find meaning and purpose at work.

henning-showkeir & associates, inc. was founded by the late Joel Henning and Jamie Showkeir in 2000 to fulfill this promise. Maren Showkeir joined the business as a managing partner in 2005. We work from the perspective of distributing organizational power and creating partnership as a strategy for managing an enterprise.

Our consulting strategy is to deliver our expertise in leadership development, change management, and organizational development through collaboration. We are committed to:

~ Collaborating with you in every phase of our work: design, development, implementation, and outcomes.

~ Offering you innovative, powerful methods that increase competence and accountability, tied directly to improving your business results.

~ Telling you the truth when our expertise is not relevant and helping you find the resources you need.

~ Raising difficult issues with goodwill.

Our commitment to results is always backed with a guarantee. If we don't deliver the agreed-upon results, or you don't find value in our work, you don't pay our fees.

henning-showkeir & associates, inc.
2323 N. Central Ave., #1203, Phoenix, AZ 85004
602.368.6172
www.henning-showkeir.com

Also by Maren and Jamie Showkeir

Authentic Conversations
Moving from Manipulation to Truth and Commitment

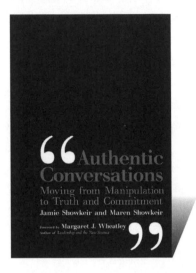

Jamie and Maren Showkeir take something people typically think of as merely functional—ordinary conversation—and show how it can lead to a workforce that is engaged and energized or to one that is alienated and uninspired. All too often workplace conversations create what the authors call parent-child relationships. People hide facts, sugarcoat reality, and claim helplessness to try to control the interaction and get what they want. The Showkeirs demonstrate how we can move to honest and authentic adult conversations that create increased commitment, true accountability, and improved business performance. They provide a hands-on guide, including sample scripts, for dealing with a host of potentially difficult conversations.

Paperback, 240 pages, ISBN 978-1-57675-595-2
PDF ebook, ISBN 978-1-57675-981-3

BK Berrett–Koehler Publishers, Inc.
San Francisco, *www.bkconnection.com*   **800.929.2929**

Berrett–Koehler
Publishers

Berrett-Koehler is an independent publisher dedicated to an ambitious mission: *Creating a World That Works for All*.

We believe that to truly create a better world, action is needed at all levels—individual, organizational, and societal. At the individual level, our publications help people align their lives with their values and with their aspirations for a better world. At the organizational level, our publications promote progressive leadership and management practices, socially responsible approaches to business, and humane and effective organizations. At the societal level, our publications advance social and economic justice, shared prosperity, sustainability, and new solutions to national and global issues.

A major theme of our publications is "Opening Up New Space." Berrett-Koehler titles challenge conventional thinking, introduce new ideas, and foster positive change. Their common quest is changing the underlying beliefs, mindsets, institutions, and structures that keep generating the same cycles of problems, no matter who our leaders are or what improvement programs we adopt.

We strive to practice what we preach—to operate our publishing company in line with the ideas in our books. At the core of our approach is stewardship, which we define as a deep sense of responsibility to administer the company for the benefit of all of our "stakeholder" groups: authors, customers, employees, investors, service providers, and the communities and environment around us.

We are grateful to the thousands of readers, authors, and other friends of the company who consider themselves to be part of the "BK Community." We hope that you, too, will join us in our mission.

A BK Life Book

This book is part of our BK Life series. BK Life books change people's lives. They help individuals improve their lives in ways that are beneficial for the families, organizations, communities, nations, and world in which they live and work. To find out more, visit **www.bk-life.com**.

Berrett–Koehler
BK Publishers

A community dedicated to creating
a world that works for all

Visit Our Website: www.bkconnection.com

Read book excerpts, see author videos and Internet movies, read
our authors' blogs, join discussion groups, download book apps, find
out about the BK Affiliate Network, browse subject-area libraries of
books, get special discounts, and more!

Subscribe to Our Free E-Newsletter, the *BK Communiqué*

Be the first to hear about new publications, special discount offers,
exclusive articles, news about bestsellers, and more! Get on the list
for our free e-newsletter by going to **www.bkconnection.com**.

Get Quantity Discounts

Berrett-Koehler books are available at quantity discounts for orders
of ten or more copies. Please call us toll-free at (800) 929-2929 or
email us at bkp.orders@aidcvt.com.

Join the BK Community

BKcommunity.com is a virtual meeting place where people from
around the world can engage with kindred spirits to create a world
that works for all. **BKcommunity.com** members may create their own
profiles, blog, start and participate in forums and discussion groups,
post photos and videos, answer surveys, announce and register for
upcoming events, and chat with others online in real time. Please join
the conversation!